On
Evil

. . . the author actually does what too few academics do: exhibit thought in action, not substituting the stale cite for an original idea.

Fred Alford, author of *What Evil Means to Us*

Praise for the series

"... allows a space for distinguished thinkers to write about their passions"

The Philosophers' Magazine

"... deserves high praise"

Boyd Tonkin, The Independent (UK)

"This is clearly an important series. I look forward to reading future volumes."

Frank Kermode, author of Shakespeare's Language

"... both rigorous and accessible"

Humanist News

"... the series looks superb"

Quentin Skinner

"... an excellent and beautiful series"

Ben Rogers, author of A.J. Ayer: A Life

"Routledge's *Thinking in Action* series is the theory junkie's answer to the eminently pocketable Penguin 60s series."

Mute Magazine (UK)

"Routledge's new series, *Thinking in Action*, brings philosophers to our aid ..."

Evening Standard (UK)

"... a welcome new series by Routledge"

Bulletin of Science, Technology and Society

ADAM MORTON

On
Evil

Routledge
Taylor & Francis Group

NEW YORK AND LONDON

First published 2004
by Routledge
711 Third Avenue, New York, NY 10017

Simultaneously published in the UK
by Routledge
2 Park Square, Milton Park, Abingdon, Oxon, OX14 4RN

Routledge is an imprint of the Taylor & Francis Group

Typeset in Joanna MT and DIN by
RefineCatch Ltd, Bungay, Suffolk

Library of Congress Cataloging in Publication Data
Morton, Adam.
    On evil / Adam Morton. – 1st ed.
        p.   cm. – (Thinking in action)
    Includes bibliographical references and index.
    1. Good and evil. I. Title. II. Series.
    BJ1401 .M67   2004
    170–dc22   2003026285

British Library Cataloguing in Publication Data
A catalogue record for this book is available from the British Library

ISBN 0–415–30518–7 (hbk)
ISBN 0–415–30519–5 (pbk)

Then for the first time, we became aware that our language lacks words to express this offence, the demolition of a man.

Primo Levi, *If This Is a Man* (1959)

The greatest evil is not now done in those sordid "dens of crime" that Dickens loved to paint. It is not done even in concentration camps and labor camps. In those we see its final result. But it is conceived and ordered (moved, seconded, carried, and minuted) in clean, carpeted, warmed, and well-lighted offices, by quiet men with white collars and cut fingernails and smooth-shaven cheeks who do not need to raise their voice.

C. S. Lewis, Preface to *The Screwtape Letters* (1961)

This is a book about how we can understand the awful things people do. My main inspiration for this book has not been the philosophers and theologians who have reflected on the meaning of evil. I am a professional philosopher and I have read much of this literature. But I must say that it has given me much less of a grasp of what lies behind atrocity than the work of the witnesses, people such as Hannah Arendt, Gitta Sereny, Primo Levi, Alexsandr Solzhenitsyn, and Desmond Tutu, who have undergone or had to deal with atrocity first hand. One of the legacies of the twentieth century is the reflections of such people. I have also learned a lot from recent psychological work on dangerous people. So this book is a philosopher's reaction to the work of those who have observed, in real life or the laboratory, evil motives at work. It is not a reflection on any central texts of our culture. It does not take a traditional concept of evil, supposed to be a fixed target, and try to say something deep about it. I am convinced, in fact, that that is precisely what we should not do. Instead it asks "How should we think about the atrocities around us? What concepts do we need, if we are to know how to explain and how to react?"

The main text avoids scholarly disputes and complications. The notes at the end of the book refer to sources and debates. When something I say seems wrong or mysterious, you might look at the notes for that section. I have had wonderfully helpful comments on drafts of this book from Susanna Braund, Tony Bruce, Neera Badhwar, Susanne Bobzien, Ruth Garrard, Peter Goldie, and Shaun Nichols. An American Philosophical Association symposium on Claudia Card's *The Atrocity Paradigm* in May 2003 widened my perspective dramatically. My senior seminar in the spring of 2003 at the University of Oklahoma was invaluable for trying out ideas and discovering the range of reactions to facts and theories about human awfulness. Each of the twenty-four students has influenced some part of this book.

One

We're in the midst of it, as always. Human beings are committing atrocities upon one another with the same enthusiasm or carelessness that has always marked our species. When we think of evil we think first of large-scale horrors. We think of the Holocaust in Europe, the Gulags of Stalin's USSR, of Cambodia and Rwanda. But equally horrifying things happen on a smaller scale. As I write young women are disappearing regularly in the Mexican state of Juarez, murdered by some systematic and as yet unknown group. A newspaper article reports that in South Africa sixty children a day are raped, some of them less than a year old. In Britain and the Middle East women who are seen to have dishonored their families are frequently murdered. In the United States school and workplace shootings are far from uncommon. And these must be taken against the background of isolated everyday murders, rapes, tortures, and assaults that has always been part of life everywhere.

There is something deeply puzzling about this. Why do people do these things? We can be puzzled at our own past actions. How could I have done that? The puzzlement focuses on acts that impose death, pain, or humiliation on others, on atrocities. We find it much harder to understand how people can do these things when they involve atrocity than when it is a matter "merely" of fraud, deception, or broken promises. We find the origins of atrocity so puzzling that we label the mystery Evil, and we grope desperately for explanations of it. One way we try to understand it is to refer new cases back to a few familiar images of evil. When President Bush on January 29, 2002 referred to an "axis of evil," he was combining everyone's reactions to the events of September 11, 2001 with an allusion to the opposed ideologies of the Second World War. He was comparing the states that he took to be abetting terrorism to a popular image of demonic storm troopers, concentration camp guards, and invading Japanese armies. The comparison is disturbingly like the one that Iranian clerics used in November of 1979 when, in justifying taking US diplomats hostage, they characterized America as "the great Satan," the demonic source of evil in the world.

This book is about evil and our capacities for understanding it. I shall argue that there is indeed something special about evil, psychologically and morally. We need to distinguish a special class of horrible actions whose causes are different in important ways from those of other wrongdoing, and to which the right reactions are also different. But I shall also argue that demonic images of evil, those that make the psychology of evil totally different from that of normal human motivation, are a trap. Not only are the extreme forms of these images, according to which the perpetrators are moved by factors beyond human comprehension, wrong, but we also have reason to avoid more nuanced forms, which see very distinctive abnormal motivational patterns behind most awful behavior. By the end of the book I hope to have convinced you that most evil acts are performed by people disturbingly like you and me, that we can have some imaginative grasp on what it is like to perform many evil acts, and that in doing so we have to understand some very basic and important facts about human motivation. I shall describe some shifts of the imagination which give us a better hold on our own and other people's potentialities for evil.

In arguing for these conclusions I am both drawing on and disagreeing with traditions in psychology and philosophy. It is indeed remarkable how little discussion of extreme wrongdoing there has been in the history of philosophy. With the exception of Nietzsche, the primary focus of most moral philosophers has been on wrongs whose motives are pretty easy to grasp. Telling a lie in order to gain money, breaking a promise because the circumstances have changed, killing a rival for power or love. Some of these acts are very wrong, and some may even be evil, but in order to understand them one does not have to engage with the depths of human depravity. Yet the philosopher Kant, for example, treats it as a deep and indeed insoluble mystery why anyone would do anything as unreasonable as lie to escape embarrassment. An alien reading the history of western philosophy could get the impression that our species is generally composed of reasonable people who sometimes make a mistake in calculating what is in the common good, and sometimes put their own interest above others, but otherwise all share the same motivation. Psychologists, on the other hand, are interested in pathological behavior, and have classified violent and dangerous personalities, their developmental paths, and treatments that succeed or more often fail in taming them. From reading the psychologists an alien might get the impression that our species is riddled with unpredictably dangerous and irrational individuals. From both the philosophers and the psychologists one could get the impression that we, the normal people who occasionally stray off the straight and narrow, are fundamentally different from the pathologically dangerous people studied by the psychology of deviance, whose actions lie behind the atrocities all around us. This is wrong. The average reader of this book is not unimaginably different from many of the perpetrators of evil deeds, and a large proportion of the evil in the world is the result of the actions of people well within the range of normal routines of social life. Or so I shall argue.

HOW "EVIL" MAKES EVIL

First, a warning. There is a strong case to be made for distrusting the very idea of Evil. Thinking in terms of evil may lead to confusion and indeed to more awful consequences. That is the case against evil, and I must begin by making it.

"Evil" is part of the vocabulary of hatred, dismissal, or incomprehension. We call acts or people evil when they are so bad that we cannot fit them within our normal moral and explanatory frames. To call what Hitler or Pol Pot did "wrong" seems to understate its nature almost to the point of error; so we pull out a special term of beyond-the-pale condemnation and call them "evil." We do the same for many rapists or abusers of children: our horror drives us to a special terminology. In so doing we signal to the world our horror. We say "I react to this with simple uncomplicated condemnation, putting aside excuses and forgiveness." But of course we rarely think of ourselves in these terms. We think of ourselves as rarely straying too far from decency, and when we do stray, we think we know the reasons why. We cannot imagine participating in genocide or in the sadistic rape of a child. So, we think, the psychology behind these acts must be very different from ours; they must come from reasons we can hardly grasp, which put them beyond the scope of ordinary understanding and into a category of wrongdoing that lies beyond any possibility of excuse.

But if the motives for evil acts are so different from our everyday moral and less moral motives, then the people who commit these acts must be very different from us. They must be evil people. So we are pushed towards explaining why so many horrible things happen by supposing that there is a minority of humans whose minds work in a very different way to those of the rest of us, without whom the world would be a much safer and less appalling place. We are pushed to a kind of virtuous paranoia.

The paranoia has bad effects. The most dramatic effect is the permission it gives for reprisals, witch-hunts, protective or pre-emptive atrocities. We have social and emotional barriers against harming our fellow humans. The most fundamental is against killing them. When we categorize people as fundamentally unlike the rest of us, we make it easier to overcome those barriers. (The factors that allow us to overcome barriers in our treatment of others play a large role in later chapters of this book. They are central to chapter two.) So we can do things to them that we would normally shrink from. We can inflict evils on them.

There are also subtler dangers to thinking in terms of evil. Much of the misery of the world is caused by the thoughtlessness, callousness, or ignorance of perfectly ordinary people, acting in ways that we could not easily classify as evil. Much misery happens not because a small number of people act out of hatred or sadism but because a large number of people act with limited care or imagination. And many real horrors are the result of the intelligent choices of people we could not easily call evil. (I say more about this in "Truman versus Milosevic" below.) Thinking in terms of evil can make it harder to see this: we are pushed to thinking that awful things result from awful motives, to placing the blame for horrors on those whose motives we can see as awful and alien.

Contemporary social psychology has a name for the mistake we make here. We fall into "the fundamental attribution error" when we underestimate how much each person's behavior varies from one situation to another. We explain why sometimes we meet one kind of behavior – lying, truth-telling, or cooperation, or whatever – and sometimes another by thinking that some people lie, or tell the truth or cooperate, most of the time and others do not. But in fact each person's actions vary more from occasion to occasion than we normally suppose, so that the variation in the acts we observe is due more to each person's variability and less to the variety of people around us. Thinking in terms of evil can amount to falling into just this fallacious pattern. When we see awful acts or atrocious situations we look for the consistently awful people who must be behind them.

The danger is this. Thinking in terms of evil can give us the same attitudes as evil-doers. They often think their victims deserve what they get, that they are worthless scum, inferior beings, or dangerously alien. They often think, in fact, that their victims are evil. Thinking in terms of evil can, if we are not careful, make us accomplices in atrocity.

HOW TO BEGIN

"But there *are* psychopaths, serial killers, and terrorists, and they *do* think in different ways from the rest of us." Yes, but note two things. First, to admit that there are particular dangerous or horrifying personalities is not to say that they are dangerous in similar ways. A serial rapist-killer and a suicide bomber, for example, are likely to be as different from each other as either is from an average well-behaved citizen of Kansas City. And, second, to say that these people are different from the rest of us is not to say in what ways they are different, and how different they are, and what role their acts play in producing the evils around us. But in spite of these qualifications, the answer has to be Yes. There are some very dangerous people, few enough and separate enough from the mainstream of society that we often do not appreciate their dangerousness until it is too late. And there are unspeakably awful events, in which people for no fault of their own undergo horrors we can hardly imagine; and there are more of these than we can bear to admit. It's a very rough world.

How can we do justice to both sides of the coin? How can we find a way of acknowledging the roughness of the world, and the psychology of its more dangerous inhabitants, without falling into the paranoid trap of thinking that there is a special kind of hideous person whose motives are quite different from those of normal people, and whose actions are at the heart of the awful situations around us? I suggest three conditions on a theory of evil: three tests for it to meet. If a theory does not pass the tests, then it has not acquitted "evil" of the doubts expressed in the previous section; it has not shown that we would not be better off banning the term from serious uses.

1 Comprehension. Instead of depicting the motives of evil-doers as unintelligible, an enlightening theory of evil should help us to understand the variety of motives for performing evil actions, and the varied resemblances these motives have to those that operate in normal human life. It should expand our resources for understanding one another.

2 *Banality.* A theory of evil should be consistent with the fact that many horrors, particularly large-scale, society-wide horrors such as the Holocaust, require the interaction of a variety of personalities. And among these personalities some are marked not by viciousness but by traits that would in other circumstances lead them to be useful members of society. So, whether or not Hannah Arendt was right that large-scale totalitarian evil is characterized by such banality, there is little doubt that many participants in evil are not moved by extraordinary hatred or sadism. We shall return to the issue in chapter 3.

3 *Reflexiveness.* A theory of evil should help us to understand how *we* can be seen as evil. People who thought of themselves as patriots are often amazed that others see them as war criminals; people who thought of themselves as defenders of decency are amazed that others see them as bigots; people who see themselves as productive members of society are amazed that others see them as implicated in the misery of others. And, in particular, members of rich western societies, Americans possibly more than others, find it almost incomprehensible how others in the world can think of some of their core motives as deeply reprehensible. These are shifts of moral perspective that require an enormous amount of understanding or imagination. A good theory of evil should give us some help in making these shifts.

In this book I shall try to put together an account of evil that meets these three conditions. I shall draw together insights from a large number of philosophers, psychologists, and other thinkers, in a way that emphasizes issues about our abilities to understand one another. An account of evil is in part an account of why people do evil things, and how much of evil motivation can be grasped with our natural intuitive understanding of one another. There is a deep and delicate relation between intuitive psychological understanding and moral judgment. In particular we find it extremely hard to make two leaps of imagination: to see the motivation of someone who has done something appalling, and to see how someone could be appalled by something we have done with a clear conscience. The kind of philosophy I aim at should expand our capacities to make such leaps.

EVIL VERSUS WRONG

I am looking for an honest and enlightening account of evil. To be honest it must recognize that there are many different reasons why people do terrible things and that there are many different ways in which a situation can be terrible, and it must be based on our best current psychology rather than on folklore. But to be enlightening it must make connections between some of these different motives and situations. The first thing we need is some hold on what does and does not count as evil. In this section I shall contrast what is evil with what is "merely" bad or wrong.

We use the word "evil" to pick out particular kinds of wrong actions and their bad consequences. But not all very wrong actions are evil. And some acts have the main features of evil acts though they are not very wrong. In fact, one act can be more wrong than another but less evil. This is a subtle business; we have to tease out what distinction we are making when we describe an act as evil rather than just wrong. Consider three imaginary examples. In all three we can describe a person's act so that it is on the border between evil and some other kind of wrongdoing. In each case there is something to be learned from the further factors that tilt it nearer to or further away from evil.

The first example is a case of serious negligence. Suppose that I am in charge of a famine relief project and I mismanage the fuel supplies for the planes that parachute food to people in the desert. I thoughtlessly put them where corrupt warlords can seize them. The planes cannot fly, the food is not delivered, and people starve. I feel guilty, as I have allowed these people to die. The administrators running the project have doubts about whether I should be employed.

I have a lot to answer for. Contrast my faults, though, with those of the people who stole the fuel. They are killers. They have very different faults from mine. Are they worse? It is often pointless to debate which of two crimes is greater. But in this case it seems clear that for some purposes we should see my act as worse than that of the warlords. If you are trying to get the famine relief project to succeed, I am a greater menace to your aims than they are. They can be bought off, threatened, or distracted, while I am likely to cripple anything I touch with my negligence. But intuitively my motives are less evil than theirs. I have not aimed at anyone's harm, consciously or unconsciously. Though I am to blame, it is for a kind of stumbling. Notice that the more my stumbling has a pattern to it, the more it seems evil. If it turned out, for example, that I am very careful about my own affairs, and much more negligent when it is other people's interests that are at stake, then the wrong begins to have more of the smell of evil.

For a second kind of case consider someone who thinks that the only important thing in life is to be near to God, and who thinks that you can't be near to God unless you are part of her church, whose beliefs entail love and benevolence towards all humanity. She and other members of the church persuade destitute mothers around the world to give up their children to be raised in comfortable conditions by the church. Materially comfortable, that is: years later the mothers deeply regret giving up their children, and the children feel an emotional emptiness at the lack of real parents. Our person, though, has no regrets. It was all done out of love of the children, who otherwise would have had no chance of the only important thing in life. Her motives are deeply flawed, most of us will agree. There is something very wrong with her and with what she does. But it is a special kind of wrongness.

Though her acts are wrong, they are not good examples of evil. She is moved by benevolence for the very people she harms, and she does not know she is harming them. Suppose that she did have more knowledge of what effects her actions had on the children and the mothers, but kept herself from seeing the importance of these effects by repeating to herself the dogmas of her church. Then her motivation is more like that of someone who is led blindly to evil by an ideology. She would then be a cooperator in evil in a way that many well-meaning, indeed good, people are. But until we modify the story this way, her actions are better examples of doing the wrong thing than of acting evilly. (The example is based on the 2002 Australian film *Rabbit-proof Fence*, altered to make the contrast with the other examples greater.)

The third case concerns a drug company executive. His company has patented a breakthrough anti-cancer drug. A rival company has a similar drug that is almost as good, but what they don't have is our executive's discovery of a subtle loophole in the tax laws, which allows his company to avoid paying any taxes. It takes five years for the authorities to plug the loophole. During this time he plays a complex game, not reducing prices of the drug as much as he might, given the advantage over the rival, but not raising them so much that the rival gets most of the business. Instead, he lets the price of the drug dance, with the aim of always undercutting the rival slightly but also keeping the price high. It never really sinks in that the game he is playing with the rival company is costing people's lives.

Are the executive's actions evil? Well, he could be your neighbor, and he could be a conscientious member of your church and community. I think there are two ways of filling out the bare story, and in one of them his acts are evil and in the other they are not. It might be that he is just so busy, and his whole character and personality are so focused on purely commercial matters, that questions of the effect of his actions just never cross his consciousness. In that case he is a very defective person, and his actions are very wrong, but the motivation is not evil. (Imagine you are his rebellious adolescent child, searching for a wounding description. You call him a catastrophically feeble, unaware bumbler.) Suppose on the other hand that the thought that his actions are causing death does cross his mind from time to time, but whenever they do he pushes them away by focusing on the complexity of his dance with the rival company. He has a strategy for avoiding thoughts and possibilities that might make him doubt his actions. That's a kind of evil, an important and pervasive kind. (You are his rebellious child: you call him a murderer, a genocidal menace.) Self-deceptive strategies like this one play an important role in the account of evil I give in chapter two, and account for many cases of white-collar, non-violent evil.

The case was suggested by the controversy over the prices of HIV drugs in the third world. I have deliberately not made any assertions about that controversy though. The main point applies throughout commercial life: there is nothing intrinsically evil about the profit motive, but it can be a powerful tool for distracting one from the effects of one's actions.

The incompetent famine relief worker, the benevolent baby-snatcher, and the blinkered executive show ways in which one can do something very wrong that is not evil. They also show how fine this line is: they can be varied to make very similar cases in which the act is evil. So where does the line run? We should try to draw it so that without sounding too unnatural it captures an important distinction, one that is both morally and psychologically significant. In the next chapter I give a definition of evil. For now, consider three basic features of evil, that contrast it with other kinds of wrongness.

1   We have a visceral revulsion from extremely evil acts. The revulsion is most vivid when the acts involve physical violence, but it extends to other acts produced by similar patterns of motivation, even if they do not have the same emotional immediacy. Evil acts have a quality that in ancient times would have made us fear that the gods might send a plague in reprisal, rather than simply making us despair at the incapacities of mere mortals to manage their lives together.

2   Evil centers on atrocity: death, pain, and humiliation imposed on others. Evil acts produce atrocities deliberately, and with a specific kind of deliberation, in which evil-doers look away from the fact that the victims are fellow human beings. There are many ways of looking away: one of them is to think of the victims as themselves evil, or as sub-human, inferior, or disgraceful, or alternatively as enemies or foreigners.

3   The point of view of the victims of evil is usually that of incomprehension. How could anyone do this to me? There are limits to our behavior towards others that we take for granted until they are breached. This is one source of the difficulty we have imagining why people do evil things, which I discuss later in this chapter. It is also a source of the tendency of victims to blame themselves: I must have done something to deserve this.

There is a distinction behind these three features, a difference between kinds of wrongness. They bring nearer the foreground a distinction that is arguably not found in ancient culture or oriental culture, and which came into European culture with the Stoics and Christianity. It is the concept of a kind of wrongness that is deeper than the social rules we enforce to make our lives go smoothly.

Rape and torture are nearly always evil. They arouse revulsion; their perpetrators have found ways of looking away from the full nature of their acts; the victims find it hard to believe what is happening to them. Contrast this with a breach of contract. Also seriously wrong, but not revolting, not requiring twisted psychology from the perpetrator, not hard to imagine. We don't find people who have been lied to blaming themselves in desperate attempts to find an explanation of what has happened.

Adultery and other forms of sexual misconduct are interesting cases here. Adultery is sometimes evil: when it is motivated by the aim of humiliating your spouse, rather than desire for someone else. But normally it is not evil, though often seriously wrong. We do not think of adulterous couples as revolting; we do not think their actions need special explanations. We simply think, usually, that they are doing harm, breaking promises, storing up trouble for themselves and others. That is what we think, that is, if we have a contemporary attitude to sex, without the assumption that there is something intrinsically illicit about it unless protected by some social or religious sanction. If one does make some such assumption – which can be part of an attitude of the sacredness of intimate human relationships – then sexual misconduct may seem more like evil. One's disapproval may tend more towards disgust, and less towards sadness at human foolishness. (But remember Jesus. He chose an adulterous woman to make his point about the hypocrisy of condemning those who do acts one has performed in imagination. He did not choose a murderer or a rapist: his example would have fallen flat if he had.)

Rape, on this account, is usually evil because it involves a desire to humiliate the victim, to reduce her or him to the status of an object. The fact that the humiliation is sexual is incidental, though it plays on a deep human vulnerability. Consider another example. A woman persuades a man to go to bed with her by deception. She says that she has a fatal disease and that the memory she would most like to have at the end of her life is of this experience with him. Afterwards, he learns that she had no disease, and that she wanted no precious moment but simply a body that appealed to her. Should he feel as if raped? Almost everyone would say No. He should feel deceived, mistreated, used. What was done to him was wrong. But it was not evil.

Hard cases and borderline cases shouldn't be settled by fiat. There are facts to settle here, about the reactions we should have and about the reasons we do things. We should look patiently at the arguments and evidence, until we know what we want to say, and what distinctions we want to use to say it.

TRUMAN VERSUS MILOSEVIC

In July 1945 Harry Truman ordered atomic bombs to be
dropped on the Japanese cities of Hiroshima and Nagasaki.
About a hundred thousand people died, some of them
immediately and some painful lingering deaths. Soon after,
Japan surrendered. Truman's decision is usually defended on
the grounds that an American invasion of Japan would have
been enormously costly in American lives. Let us make
some reasonable assumptions, though they could be chal-
lenged. First suppose that there were alternative courses of
action that could have ended the war with smaller loss of
life. For example, an atomic bomb could have been dropped
on an unpopulated area; there was in fact a very suitable
area near Tokyo. Suppose that Truman rejected these courses
of action on inadequate grounds. Suppose, for example, that
forces within the military wanted to try out their new
bomb by really using it, and were worried by the possibility
that the Japanese might negotiate a surrender before the
bomb had been used. And think of Truman just returning
from discussing the shape of the post-war world at Potsdam
with Churchill and Stalin, swamped with all the detail con-
fronting the president of a country at war who had moreover come into the job unexpectedly not long before. So he
went along with what the generals proposed, without going
into all the details. But also suppose one other thing. Suppose that all those deaths were for him an inevitable but
very regrettable side effect. He didn't think "A lot fewer
Japanese: good." If these supposes were true, then Truman
would have acted wrongly. Very seriously wrongly: thousands died needlessly. But on this account his act is not one
of enormous evil. It is simply an enormous mistake to have
made.

Compare Harry Truman to Slobodan Milosevic. Again I am filling in details to make the example work my way. (And Milosevic is on trial as I write, so some of the facts are being contested in an adversarial fashion, something that never happened in the case of Truman. It helps to be on the winning side.) But I shall suppose the standard media version, which is that Milosevic planned a program of ethnic cleansing in Bosnia and parts of Kosovo from 1997 to 1999, in the course of which many people died and many were tortured, rapes were committed for strategic purposes, men were held in appalling conditions, subject to torture and summary execution. Probably he did not know the details of all of this, but he set in motion processes that he knew would result in such events. And he intended these horrors to fall on people because they were non-Serbians in what he took to be Serbian land. He took death, misery, and social disintegration among non-Serbians, especially Muslims, to be desirable as such. If this description is right, then Milosevic's acts are central cases of evil.

Which was worse, though, Truman's mistake or Milosevic's evil? It is often a mistake to compare horrors. It can seem to downplay how horrific the "lesser" horror is. In cases of long-running conflict, each side counts up the massacres committed by the other as if they excuse their own atrocities. Yet there is a case – I won't say more – for arguing that Truman as I have described him did something worse than the Milosevic of standard accounts. Many more people died, though fewer were made refugees, and there were more alternative means to his ends. Moreover the deaths were foreseen: it would have been possible to calculate their number to within a few hundred. And Truman was the leader of a powerful country, choosing between means to an almost inevitable victory, whose acts would set a precedent in future conflicts. Yet there is, intuitively, more evil to Milosevic and his acts than there is to Truman. So we see how there can be cases in which one act is more bad but less evil.

The same point can be made with much less dramatic cases. The three cases in the last section – the incompetent famine-reliever, the benevolent baby-snatcher, the ruthless executive – make the point. In each case the person did more harm than most rapists, serial killers, or terrorists. And in each case the person knew, or should have known, what the result of their actions would be. All of them should be held responsible, and blamed, for their acts. But blame is not a simple one-dimensional business; there are different kinds of condemnation for different kinds of wrong. We do not condemn such acts as evil, though they are wrong, and more harmful than many acts that are evil.

EVIL AND INTELLIGIBILITY

Why make such a point of separating evil from other kinds of wrong? Why make this contrast important? One reason for distinguishing things is that they call for different reactions. Compare the contrast we make between what is foolish and what is wrong. Smoking when pregnant is wrong, because someone else can be hurt. Smoking all by yourself is foolish, because you are the one who will suffer. Persuasion is the appropriate reaction to the foolish, while physical interference is often appropriate to wrongdoing. We let the former know what we think, and we do what we can to obstruct the latter.

So what are the different reactions that are appropriate to evil and to other kinds of wrong? Well, we tend to be appalled, horrified, or outraged by evil, and upset, disillusioned, or saddened by other kinds of wrong. These are only rough indicators, though: one might be appalled by the incompetent famine relief administrator, horrified by the unscrupulous executive, and outraged by the benevolent baby-snatcher. Something that underlies the differences in our reactions to evil and non-evil wrongs is a difference in our willingness to imagine what it is like to have evil motives. Suppose that you are a friend of the incompetent famine relief administrator, and you want to understand how, although he is deeply committed to alleviating the suffering of the starving people, he so often bungles the task. As you get to know him better and reflect on what it is like to be him, you get a feeling for the way he thinks. You can feel your way through problems his way, seeing where his resolve slips and where distraction seizes him. Doing this does not make you more like him. It makes you *less* like him, because it helps you avoid his mistakes. Contrast this with the prospect of getting to understand what it is like to be a serial killer or a rapist. To do this you would have to rehearse, in imagination, the absence of respect for other people as individuals, in fact the pleasure of denying that respect. It is a world one shudders to enter. Entering it imaginatively might make you more like him. Or so it feels, intuitively.

We often feel barriers to understanding acts that repel us. A fine novel by Bernhard Schlink, *The Reader* (1995), explores the connections between love, understanding, and moral judgment. The narrator loves someone who, as he learns later, has been a camp guard who has participated in a particular awful incident. He says:

> I wanted simultaneously to understand Hanna's crime and to condemn it. But it was too terrible for that. When I tried to understand it, I had the feeling I was failing to condemn it as it

> must be condemned. When I condemned it as it must be
> condemned, there was no room for understanding. But even
> as I wanted to understand Hanna, failing to understand her
> meant betraying her all over again. I could not resolve this. I
> wanted to pose myself both tasks – understanding and
> condemnation. But it was impossible to do both.

His love does not survive the discovery, or is buried by it. He also learns a number of facts that help explain why Hanna acted as she did. They could be put together to make some sort of plausible story of why someone who was not a deeply vicious person could do what she did. Schlink does not put the story together, but leaves it to the reader to construct their own version. Instead, he focuses on a more subtle issue, the tension in his narrator's mind between the need to condemn what is obviously appalling and the need to give a sympathetic explanation of the acts of someone one is close to. In chapter 4 I discuss whether some kinds of repellent acts really are harder to understand. The point now, though, is our unwillingness to try to understand them.

It is not very mysterious why we might hesitate to imagine some kinds of motivation. One reason comes from self-respect. Intuitive understanding of someone else's action usually involves imagining how you could do the same. This is near to imagining yourself doing it, which is near to imagining yourself as evil. And you want to be able to say to yourself that you are not the kind of person who could do things like that. So you don't want to learn that you can imagine being that way. In contrast, with acts that are wrong but not evil, we usually can imagine doing them by imagining that some of our actual capacities are diminished: we bracket or suspend parts of our actual psychology to do the imagining. This is not nearly as threatening an activity as adding a new element to one's psychology, or activating an unused or well-buried one.

A more subtle reason concerns the social use of explanation. We often explain what someone did in order to master a way of thinking that we can take over for our own uses. When we explain why someone did something, we see how to do it ourselves, and in thinking about how to do it we rehearse the action in our minds, becoming more capable of doing it. So when the action is evil, the explanation of it would rehearse the capacity to do it. But this is not something that we encourage. We'd prefer that the capacity to do evil things got as little rehearsal as possible.

A third reason we hesitate even to try to understand evil actions is that we fear that, if we succeeded, we might not dislike their perpetrators enough. We might be in danger of forgiving them. I think there's a mistake here: understanding and blame are often perfectly compatible. Still, there is some psychological evidence that the more people consider the possible motives for wrongdoing, the less severe their condemnation of it. It is easy to see the force of the idea: reduce the imaginative distance between yourself and evil-doers and you might find yourself sympathizing with them.

For these and other reasons we very often react to evil as if it were mysterious and inexplicable. We can't imagine how anyone like us could do anything like that. This is not a definition of evil! I'm not saying that evil acts are the ones we have barriers against understanding. It is an answer to the question why there is a point to distinguishing between evil and other kinds of wrong. One reason to make the distinction clear is that we run into different problems trying to get an intuitive handle on why people do evil acts. And to the extent that intuitive understanding of someone's action is essential to interacting with them, we are often at a loss how to respond to evil-doers. We don't know how to handle them.

THE DEMONIC IMAGE

If we hesitate to explain evil actions by referring to motives we can easily imagine, then we may be attracted to explanations that refer to exotic or supernatural motives. And what could be a better explanation of evil than the seductive influence of the devil? The devil has powers of persuasion that exceed those of any human, and their workings cannot be imagined by the unaided human mind. Moreover his whole purpose is to oppose the forces of good. And so although almost any wrongdoing can be explained in terms of the devil's influence, it is especially appropriate for making sense of actions that we cannot or do not want to explain in familiar terms.

There is a crude and a sophisticated form that the diabolical image of evil can take. In the crude form we simply imagine a realm of forces about whose motives little can be known but whose effect is to oppose anything good. The easiest ways of picturing these forces are through the mythology of demons, zombies, vampires, and the like. Each of these types is different in its characteristic way, but their similarities are more important. Each can exert a power over humans, making them aid or join them, each has a lust for something indescribably horrible, and each arouses in us reactions of terror and disgust. The imagery is at its most vivid in *Buffy the Vampire Slayer*. In each episode of the television series Buffy uses her special powers to combat terrifying and revolting supernatural agents of evil, who are often transformed human beings, in their attempts to bring horror into the lives of the inhabitants of her peaceful middle-American town. The evil beings sometimes are obvious representations of the power of sex or hatred, but their aims go infinitely further than these motives would take any normal person. In fact, we can have no grasp of their motives, other than that they aim to destroy good things in human life and to bring human beings under their control.

Contemporary mythology presents agents even more inscrutable than the undead and the possessed, namely machines. An archetypal science fiction theme is the struggle of human beings in a world dominated by machines. In films such as *The Terminator* series and *The Matrix* trilogy, human beings struggle against machines that dominate the earth. The "psychology" of these machines is completely inaccessible to humans; all we know is that they want to exterminate or enslave us. It is interesting that in order to make the action more psychologically gripping, both *Terminator* and *Matrix* feature half-way creatures: machines or computer programs with humanoid characteristics. The Schwarzenegger figures in *Terminator* films are robots in human form and with something like human motives. They are like zombies. In *The Matrix* there are "agents" of the Matrix computer, which controls human experience, who interact with humans in human form but are really subroutines of the main program with humanoid mannerisms. They are like humans possessed by alien powers. It is interesting that whether the ultimate evil is technological or metaphysical, our fantasies need something half-way human to get the glimmer of intelligibility that holds our interest.

To see the more subtle form of the diabolical image, consider the mysterious motives of demonic agents. They don't seem to be moved by desire for any particular good: they aren't aiming at their own pleasure or wealth or achievement. And this is true of many of the more appalling acts that human agents perform too: they can seem to be directed at nothing but doing wrong for its own sake. And this is puzzling: why would anyone do wrong except for the sake of something that was good, at any rate good for that person? One of the deepest and most influential meditations on this puzzle is that of Saint Augustine, writing in the last years of the Roman Empire. In his *Confessions*, Augustine reflects on pointless wrongdoing, done just for the sake of it. The central example is his own theft of pears as a youth. Modern readers often find it puzzling that such a relatively trivial matter would be Augustine's central example of sin. But his point is that the essence of sin comes out more clearly in a trivial pointless crime than in an act motivated by ambition or lust. He makes it clear that people often do wrong not for any gain to themselves but from some deeper perversity. And this is very hard to explain. As he asks, "Who can unravel that complex twisted knottedness?"

Later in the *Confessions* and in his later work *The City of God*, Augustine gives an explanation. The desire to do wrong for its own sake is the desire to oppose what is good, that is, the will of God. The model of this motive is the story of Satan himself, who was expelled from heaven because of his ambition to be as powerful as God. The aim then is perfect independence, to be subject only to one's own autonomous will. It is the aim of deciding right and wrong for oneself. Like Satan, the evil person wants to play God.

Many ambiguities and unanswered questions remain. Does the desire to be God-like make evil actions intelligible? Is it fundamentally the desire to be like God or the desire to make one's own rules? Do people do evil because of their own devilish tendencies or because of the influence of an actual devil? Augustine does not resolve all of these questions. He is clearest on the last of them. Like many Christian theologians he wrestles hard with the tension between, on the one hand, the conviction that the forces of good struggle against substantive opposition in the world, and, on the other, thinking that God is the ultimate and incomparable power. The Manichean world-view, in which the story of the world is that of the struggle between almost equal forces of good and evil, is a heresy from a Christian point of view, and Augustine had fought against it. There is nothing remotely like God. Most theologians deny the existence of the devil. So Augustine concludes that evil is due not to the influence of forces that are striving to rival God, but to the individual soul's turning away from God: "Let no one look for the efficient cause of the evil will; for it is not efficient but deficient." If he could watch an episode of Buffy, Augustine's reaction would be that the demonic characters were either hallucinations or sad damned creatures who had turned away from God, not creatures acting under the influence of a positive perverse power. (An interesting case for demonic theories among the Buffy characters is Buffy's boyfriend-enemy Angel, who has intelligible human emotions and desires but is yet committed to evil.)

There is a very basic and troubling question here for any Christian account of evil. If we don't want a secular account in which evil results from the appeal of desirable things like pleasure, love, or success, and we don't want a diabolical account in which evil results from the temptations of an almost equal anti-God, then we must trace evil to the human possibility of turning away from God. Why do we turn away? Augustine's answer is not completely clear. To some extent he thinks of it as a mystery, beyond full human comprehension. It is certainly for him part of the mysterious nature of freedom. God has given humans not only the capacity to turn freely away from him, but also a tendency to delight in the exercise of their own freedom, in whatever direction it leads them. So we are set up to be tempted by the idea of rivaling God. But why?

Whatever the answers to this might be, the suggestion that there is a link between evil and the exercise of free choice for its own sake is very attractive. Consider a story. A terrible disease is ravaging the country. Infected people are sent to special quarantine camps, where the mortality is very high. The head doctor in one such camp has sole and unchallenged authority over the distribution of the very limited supplies of a life-saving drug. He delights in deciding, on purely arbitrary grounds, who will get it. "You have thick eyebrows, I'll let you die"; "You have the same name as my favorite actress, so you'll get the cure." And what he just loves about the situation is that it's he who is deciding, and for entirely his own reasons.

What is so revolting about the doctor? He is not moved by hatred or by pleasure in the suffering of others. He is acting to save lives. The reason we think of him as evil, I suggest, is his arrogant joy in making life-and-death decisions about others, unfettered by any rules. It would be better to decide by the toss of a die than by one's whims, and to take such delight in the power of one's whims is to want to be more than any human person can be. The horror of this personality is like that of a killer stalking victims who cannot escape, for example one of the teenagers in the Columbine shootings, and deciding on the spur of the moment who to shoot and who to spare. A more everyday version of the personality is the business tycoon whose motive for building his empire is simply power, the love of being able to control others and get whatever he wants. A really big fraud would be fun not because of the additional millions but just for the sake of getting away with it. Another everyday version is the seducer, who manipulates sexual victims not for love or money or even sex, but simply to know that he has manipulated them, for the sense of power and control. An extreme fictional version of this is the character of Valmont in *Dangerous Liaisons* (*Les Liaisons dangereuses* – at least three film versions) whose predatory seductive power is simply an exercise in willfulness.

TEMPTATION

Linked to the demonic image of evil is a model of how we are tempted or seduced into evil. The Garden of Eden story says it all. Human beings were innocent until the serpent tempted Eve who tempted Adam. The idea is that a basic factor in explaining why people do wrong lies outside the individual person. There are external forces that strive towards the bad, for reasons we cannot fully understand, and which exert an influence on human choices. The model supposes we aren't motivated to perform some acts alone, but we are motivated to submit to someone else who wants us to do them. The image is in part sexual, it seems to me: an image of the desire to be dominated and made to do things that one is also revolted by. The power to which one submits can be a supernatural force, or another person, or one's own subconscious impulses.

Two images from contemporary mythology illustrate the model. In many vampire tales the vampire can appear outside your door or window, but cannot enter until you ask it in. You don't want to have your blood drained, of course, but, in the tales, you feel an awful desire to let the vampire have its way. Compare this with the dark forces in the *Star Wars* films, as personified in the vampire-like figure of Darth Vader. Darth Vader urges Luke Skywalker to "come over to the dark side," as he himself has. And Skywalker, and anyone else in close contact with Vader, feels a strong urge to submit, although what he would be submitting to is repugnant to him. The light-sabre duel between Skywalker and Vader is a representation of the struggle of the will against temptation.

There is a psychological truth here, and also something very dubious. The truth is that we can imagine wanting to be led, influenced, or manipulated to do something, even when we cannot imagine wanting to do the act towards which we are being led. The dubious aspect comes when we take this as our standard all-purpose explanation of evil motivation. In some cases *part* of the explanation of an evil action is the person's willingness to be seduced by some external force. But this willingness takes different forms in different cases, with different external forces. To suppose that that there is just one such willingness – an openness to Evil itself, the powers of darkness – is to ignore all the ways in which evil motivations differ among themselves. In the second and third chapters we shall see many such ways.

I suspect that the seduction model has its power in our culture for two reasons. One is a history of sexual repression, in which many people traditionally had many desires that they could not acknowledge, but whose presence allowed them to be manipulated by others. The power of the seducer comes from the fact that the victim wants something, but does not know what she wants, so that in yielding to him, she can satisfy her desire without having to know what its object is. But in so doing she also loses control: the acts she is led to may not be the ones she would have chosen had she known better what she wanted. The other reason is the universal appeal of rebellion. No one likes to be dominated, to be told what to do. And so there is a natural appeal in the idea of doing whatever one wants, no matter what reasons there are against it.

These two strands are very often mixed. Our literature is full of women whose sexual power leads men into acts of non-sexual wrongdoing. Eve, of course, Lady Macbeth, and very evocatively Lady Sue in Kurosawa's *Ran* (1985). And seduction can in real life be a route to evil. Crossing one boundary can make it easier to cross others. But there is a deep problem with this whole approach to evil. It faces a dilemma. It can declare that some basic human desires – for freedom, for pleasure – are intrinsically wrong. But this is morally unacceptable, I would say, since these are in themselves good things. Or it has to postulate some force that exploits our desires for freedom or pleasure to lure us into evil. But this puts us back where we started, with a mystery. I am convinced that we need take neither of these alternatives. We are pressed to accounts of evil that make people intrinsically bad or which postulate mysterious tempting forces because we look in the wrong place to understand evil. It is a mistake to look at the evil-doers' desires: they are generally like everyone else's. Instead, as I explain in chapter two, we should look at the ways their desires get turned into actions.

The big mistake, focusing on desires rather than ways of achieving them, on motives rather than motivation, can easily lead to a puritan renunciation of desire. It can also lead to the opposite twin of puritanism, the idea that in order to acknowledge what is noble in human beings, to be able to say with Nietzsche "we noble ones, we good beautiful happy ones," one also has to say with Nietzsche that "counsels for behavior in relation to . . . *dangerousness*" are "prudence, prudence, mixed with stupidity, stupidity, stupidity." That is the desperate cry of someone who wants to burst the bars of the puritan cage, because he does not understand the workings of the lock.

IMAGES AND EMOTIONS

Throughout this book I shall be arguing for continuities between normal everyday behavior and extreme evil acts. So I am arguing that evil is not such an extraordinary thing. But I am also arguing that it is a very particular thing; not all seriously wrong acts should be counted as evil. So on the level of argument I need to say carefully what I mean by evil and how it can be traced from the ordinary to the horrifying. But I also need to persuade at another level, that of emotional reaction and graspable image. For I have to make you think that the concept I am describing is worth identifying with the resonant name of Evil, and that the continuities I am describing can give you new ways of thinking about motives and judgments.

There is another way of putting this. My project here is related to a general movement in psychology and philosophy to find ways of talking about our emotions that break with the old picture of emotion as an uncontrollable irrational factor that perturbs our efforts to live successful lives. Thus in philosophy there is a lot of contemporary discussion of the rationality of the emotions, of the way that some emotions can make more sense in given circumstances than others. And in psychology there is the idea of emotional intelligence, the capacity to feel the emotions that the situation demands. The idea behind both is that we should aim at becoming people who have in their repertoire a range of emotions, which will contain a suitable reaction to most situations we encounter. In discussing evil I am concerned with emotions of outrage, horror, and fury, also reconciliation and despair. I want to be part of a search for emotions that allow us to come to terms with the awfulness of human behavior.

But there is an obstacle to any attempt to be articulate and revisionary about emotions. The currency of our emotions is images, stereotypes, simple scenarios. These are stubborn and conservative things: they don't change easily and they tend to embody traditional, often primordial, ways of thinking. In the case of evil, we have images of diabolical cruelty and of deeply perverse commitment to badness. These images stand in the way of the continuities I want to trace. They apply only to extreme cases. But I cannot simply ignore them; for then what I say would have little impact where it really matters, in our range of emotional reactions to atrocity. So throughout the book I shall pay a lot of attention to popular images of evil, especially in fiction and film.

Notice to my fellow philosophers: you can be as lucid and incisive as you want, but you're not going to change the way many people think unless you give them helpful images, simple story-frames, appealing labels.

To end this first chapter, then, I shall mention two further ways in which images of evil interact with atrocity itself. I have described the dangerous self-fulfilling quality of the concept of evil: it allows us to label others in a way that suspends our sense of their humanity. The demonic image of evil is worryingly well suited for this role.

Worse, the demonic image supports mutual evil-labeling. For if there is no possibility of understanding someone, then there is much less point in entering into a complex inter-action with them. You don't do business with someone who is a complete mystery to you. You just act to protect yourself; you minimize your possible losses. You don't reveal much about your own motives, and the other is likely to think of you as uncooperative and hard to understand. This is often the case with hostile ethnic groups. Members of each group will act to others in the group in ways that make clear what they want and how they think, but with members of the other group they will mask their feelings. So each group will think of the other as hard to understand. Each will *be* hard to understand, because each is convinced that the other will not understand them.

There is another way the demonic image can lead to evil itself. Although it may be very hard to understand the attractive power of doing evil itself, the attractive power of an *image* of evil is a lot easier to understand. So although there have long been people who killed numbers of people over a period of time, now anyone who fits that description thinks of themselves as a serial killer, conscious of the image presented in films and novels. And we can begin to understand how living up to that label could fill some person's deep need.

In the same way, a person can think of another as in some way evil, and can admire and emulate them, while thinking of their model's psychology as completely inscrutable. One can worship the devil, or admire Hitler. And the less real the psychological insight that comes with the image the better it can serve this role. For the more that the image represents an actual imaginable personality, the harder it is to identify with the image unless one does in fact have that personality. If the image is completely accurate, then trying to live up to it will add nothing.

Of course the motives for emulating an evil model are usually very mixed. Saddam Hussein's worship of Stalin was in part an admiration for his tactics for suppressing rivals and mastering a population. But there is also the thought, "in some mysterious way this person managed to bring dread to

all who knew him: if I take him as a model, so may I."
Though there are no devils, people's beliefs in devils can be a
powerful force for evil.

If our aim is to think more clearly about evil, we are searching for a psychologically accurate and morally helpful image
of evil motivation. An image that is not accurate condemns us
to misunderstanding the causes of horribly important events.
It can make us underestimate our own potentialities for evil.
An image that is morally unhelpful can, among other things,
perpetuate the very atrocious phenomena it characterizes.
And yet an image that promises too easy understanding
makes evil motivation seem ordinary, and thus threatens to
undermine moral condemnation. We need to keep some of
the sense of otherness, that evil actions come from something
different than our everyday activities, even from most of our
everyday morally imperfect activities. We need an accurate
image of a specific kind of otherness.

Two

In recent decades many psychologists have studied the factors that make people dangerous or socially deviant. They have made significant discoveries. It would be wrong to represent this work as the psychology of evil. For one thing, the research makes it clear how many different ways someone can be or become a menace. I begin with an exposition of the psychology. Then I can present my theory, the barrier theory of evil, which characterizes evil actions in terms of mental procedures that find ways around our barriers against harm. The barrier theory is philosophy; it takes the wide variety of motivational patterns that underlie kinds of behavior that we intuitively think of as evil, and finds common factors not in terms of the causes of these patterns but in terms of moral judgment and intuitive understanding.

VIOLENCE

Begin with the psychology of violence. We are non-violent most of the time. Most social interactions of most people involve no use of physical force. But every person is potentially violent, and some people are violent in a significant proportion of their dealings with others. In fact, violence or the threat of it is central to some people's strategy for coping with life. These are violent individuals. The difference between violent individuals and average human beings living in well-ordered societies is dramatic, both in the extreme propensity to violence of some such individuals and in the remarkable resistance to violence of most others. One index of this fact is that several studies show that in infantry combat a significant proportion of soldiers never fire at an individual enemy soldier. This is a situation that one might expect to overcome almost anyone's barriers against injuring another: those are the enemy, after all, and you've been given very explicit encouragement to harm them, and above all they are trying to kill you. But even then, many people hesitate, unable to cross the threshold.

This is not to say that violence is alien to human nature. We are not a sweet and peaceful species. In many situations more violent behavior will win over less violent, even when the results of less violent interaction are better for both parties. So a person who did not have violence among her options would be at a significant disadvantage. But a society in which individuals exercised this option too readily would not thrive, in comparison with one in which the stakes have to be high before physical damage is a possibility. So we can expect that people will have two modes, peaceful and violent, with the peaceful mode as the norm and a transition to violence that can be triggered by various factors. The trigger can be more sensitive in some people than in others.

This picture is confirmed by studies of the development of violent personalities. There are obviously many variations on the basic patterns, but running through them there is usually a thread with the following elements. Early in childhood the individual is subject to or threatened by violence, usually from physically abusive family members or a dangerous way of life. Later in childhood but usually before adolescence the individual discovers the advantages of developing an image as someone prone to violence: as requiring less than average provocation before resorting to effective physical assault. The discovery is usually made as the result of occasions on which crossing the threshold pays off dramatically. Then, later in life, as a teenager or young adult, the image sinks in and becomes integrated with the rest of the personality. We now have a person whose way of managing social situations is based on the routine use of violence and transparent threats of violence. This person now has a route over the threshold between the pacific and the violent modes, a route which they will take more and more often, and which has become essential to their functioning.

This process is often called "violentization." Perhaps any of us could have been violentized, given suitable early history. Perhaps some individuals are more susceptible to it than others, though even these individuals require the process in order to become dangerous. It does suggest a way in which violence is passed down from one generation to another: violent individuals create an atmosphere of fear in which some children discover their own capacity for violence and eventually become violent adults. There are two components of this transmission. The most obvious is the use of violence in family life. A more subtle one is an atmosphere of fear and the availability of a set of self-images which can mediate the transition from a normal social manner to a physically aggressive one. One factor that can encourage such an atmosphere is the self-image of a group or nation as victims, as having been defeated or mistreated in the past in a way that gives permission for violence that can be seen as a defense of the group's very survival. In this way a family, an ethnic group, or a nation as a whole can be in something like the position of a child who has suffered at the hands of powerful adults and is beginning to reshape itself as someone who cannot be pushed around.

The violentization process I have just described begins in childhood and has done its work when the adult personality is being formed. A related process can operate on adults who do not have a childhood history of abuse and aggression. The model case is that of combatants' post-traumatic stress disorder. The pattern is described eloquently in Jonathan Shay's *Achilles in Vietnam* (1994). Shay, a psychiatrist who specializes in the treatment of war veterans and who also has a deep knowledge of classical literature, argues for a standard route to the classic post-combat personality disturbances. These disturbances cover a wide range of symptoms, including inability to sleep, inability to trust others, fear of open spaces, abuse of alcohol and other drugs, and most of all, a tendency to erupt into violent rage on very little provocation. Shay argues that these are symptoms that warriors have exhibited in the aftermath of war since the days of Homer. The route that leads to this destination begins with adults, usually adults with no greater propensity to violence than others from their societies. These adults are put in situations of enormous physical danger and experience great fear. Often they also experience the incompetence or betrayal of those in command. One result is a very tight bonding, love, between the men who have to rely on one another for survival. When, as often, this is followed by the death of a brother-in-war, the result is intense rage. One consequence of such rage is that the individual enters a "berserker" state in which he has superhuman strength and awareness and an inhuman disregard for personal danger. If he survives the dangers which he exposes himself to in this state, he gets the impression that he can become invulnerable by going berserk. And then eventually, if he continues to survive, he faces the transition back to civilian life.

Shay's subtitle is "Combat trauma and the undoing of character." The word "undoing" is significant. Warriors undergo the process later in life than children in the classic violentization process. They come to it with personalities already formed, and as a result they are not well placed to integrate into their personalities the violent tendencies they acquire. The ex-berserkers are invariably disturbed and unhappy people. (A "standard" violent personality, on the other hand, need not be unhappy or dysfunctional: just very bad news for those around him.) The important similarity between combat veterans suffering from post-traumatic stress disorder and violent individuals is that both have found a route, a potentially habitual route, across the barriers between pacific and violent behavior. What we learn from both cases is that these barriers are usually high enough that most normal humans do not regularly overcome them, that one can learn to overcome them, and that what one has learned is very hard to unlearn.

Note that I have not described anyone as evil – yet. Violentization and post-traumatic stress can both lead to evil actions. But they can have many other results too.

TRANSITIONS

The transition between pacific and violent mode is made for a reason, though sometimes a slight one. Visualize this as follows. The pacific mode is a horizontal line extending all the way to the left and ending somewhere in the middle. The violent mode is a horizontal line higher up (at a higher level of aggression, if you will) extending all the way to the right and also ending somewhere in the middle, but to the left of where the first line ends, so that there is a region where the first line is underneath the second. Moving from left to right we get situations of increasing provocation. At some point in the overlap region, the person's state jumps from the lower line to the upper. And moving from right to left on the upper line, there comes a point for each person at which their state jumps down to the lower line: even the most enraged individual will calm down given a sufficient absence of provocation. The more violent a personality is, the sooner, coming from the left, the leap up to the violent mode will be made, and the later, coming from the right, the drop down to pacific mode will be made. The points at which the two transitions occur will not be the same. Typically the point for the upward leap will be to the right of the point for the downward drop. This happens in everyday life: you can tolerate the dog barking and shop people being sullen and even your boss telling you off. Then you discover that a much less competent and experienced coworker has got a promotion instead of you. You are in a rage, and in that state the boss, the shop people, and even the dog will be intolerable.

This asymmetry between making a transition between modes in two directions is a general feature of human and

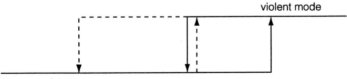

Transition points between peaceful and violent modes of behavior: the appropriateness of violence increases from left to right. Solid arrows mark the points where a normal person shifts mode; dotted arrows where a more violent person might shift.

animal emotions. A person with perfect emotional control would respond appropriately to their situation, and would have very little asymmetry: the transitions in either direction would occur at almost the same points. But normal human beings are not like this, and as a result we can ratchet up our tendencies to violence. Suppose that a person is in an aggressive state and is then exposed to a situation that would not be sufficient to make him aggressive had he not already been. But he is, and so he reacts aggressively to the situation. Suppose it pays off. Then he may learn to be aggressive given less provocation than previously, and the area of overlap between pacific and violent modes moves "leftwards" towards milder provoking situations.

Most of the time it is in the interest of humanity as a whole that most people behave non-violently. And yet it is important to keep the potentiality in reserve for when it is needed. So it is useful for there to be a certain amount of social pressure on one another to make the transition to violence only when appropriate. The standards of appropriateness will vary from one society to another, and it has been argued that in some violent societies something like the violentization process has been part of a normal development. Still, we need to know who has violent tendencies, and when they are likely to be elicited. So it is not surprising that humans are quite sensitive to this aspect of one another's behavior. It seems, in fact, that from an early age children can judge when an act of aggression is inappropriate.

This is one part of a profound discovery by the psychologist Elliot Turiel (1983). Turiel discovered that pre-school children can distinguish between two kinds of things one should not do: those that are so for reasons of social convention and those that are so for more fundamental reasons. A standard example of the first is a boy's wearing a dress to school; kindergarten children will generally say that a boy should not do this, but will also say that in a school where this was explicitly allowed it would be alright. A standard example of the second is a child hitting another child; the children will say that a child should not do this, but will also say that a child should not do it even if it was explicitly allowed. What the children understand is that there are some things for which permission cannot be given.

Part of the interest of Turiel's discovery is that small children have no problem with a distinction that philosophers and social psychologists have difficulty recreating. The discovery fits, though, with other ideas about the nature of our capacities for social life. It is widely believed among psychologists and theorists of human evolution that we are born with dispositions to develop capacities for living and cooperating with others. Among them are sensitivity to fairness and unfairness in the distribution of food and other resources, and to cheating in claims and distribution. And among these capacities is that of recognizing when violence is inappropriate. So – though I don't believe exactly these questions have been used in experiments – if children were asked whether it would be wrong to punch a thief who was stealing a child's toys, we can expect them to say that it is not wrong, although it would be wrong for one child to punch another in the course of taking his toys.

One thing that Turiel's work suggests, then, is that the awareness of whether another's liability to violence is appropriate is deeply ingrained in us, and that we very easily link this awareness to norms of behavior that we treat very seriously. The most natural explanation of this is that it has always been in our interest to maintain a social pressure to keep one another on the gentle side of violence, except on those occasions when another mode of behavior is called for.

Our sensitivity to inappropriate violence meshes very nicely with a suggestion of another psychologist. Robert Blair's studies of violent criminals suggest to him that in normal individuals there is a specific mechanism, which Blair calls the VIM (violence inhibiting mechanism), which serves to suppress impulses to react violently to current situations. More specifically, the VIM is sensitive to signs of distress in others and in their presence inhibits aggressive behavior. (It is analogous to the inhibitions that prevent wolves from tearing one another apart, but in wolves the signs are of submission and in humans they are of distress.) And since the first hints of likely violence will usually evoke signs of distress, the effect will be to prevent these first hints from developing into full-fledged aggression. So, to use the image above, the VIM prevents an individual's state from making the leap to the upper line until the situation has moved a long way to the right. The neurological roots of the mechanism are conjectured to be innate, and indeed there is some evidence of specific neurological damage that is correlated with violent behavior.

The VIM is an inbuilt piece of mental machinery. In some people it is damaged or absent. Could it be replaced? One way of reading Anthony Burgess's novel *A Clockwork Orange* (and the 1971 Stanley Kubrick film) is as a description of an attempted VIM-replacement. The "hero," Alex, lives for the joy of violence. He is "cured" by a process of conditioning which associates nausea with violent impulses. Immediately after the treatment (before the plot takes some other turns), rape, assault, murder, his former joys, are simply impossible for him. So you might think he was now an approximation to a normal human being. But no, he is an incompetent mess: he cannot defend himself, he cannot even signal that he might defend himself, so that he is a walking invitation to violence from others. Our natural innate inhibitions are far from perfect, but they are flexible. They aim to be sensitive to when aggression is appropriate and when it is not. Since we need our aggressiveness, as our ancestors did, we need sensitive ways of inhibiting it. Sensitive machinery easily goes wrong.

For most of us it is not easy to suppress or bypass the inhibition to violence. Many soldiers never shoot to kill. It takes a lot to get us to make the transition. Yet some people clearly make it terrifyingly readily. Some people are probably born with a hair-trigger to their rage mechanism, but we can imagine how the mechanism can get re-set. Compare the violence inhibition to some others. People normally have some fear of heights, as of other dangers – large carnivores, well-equipped insects – and of some harmless things – corpses, moonlight. But exposure to situations in which one has to tolerate these fears leads in many cases to a suppression of the fear, and to a special kind of pleasure, which depends on the fact that its object once terrified one. So try this comparison for thinking of what it is like to be a violent person. As a child you were afraid of heights, and wouldn't walk along a plank between barrels. But your father forced you to accompany him to the edges of canyons, then to clamber down and up steep hillsides, then to rappel down cliffs and cross ravines on teetering rope bridges. At each stage something in you screamed, but at each stage you ignored the scream and made yourself do it. And after each occasion you had a strangely elated sensation, not from the experience of the heights but from the satisfaction of facing down your terror. And then eventually you have changed, so that you can agree with the mountaineer Joe Simpson in his book *The Game of Ghosts* (1994):

There is a perverse delight in putting oneself in a potentially dangerous situation, knowing that your experience and skill make you quite safe. . . . As you step up on the first hold or drive the first axe blow, you step into a new perspective, a world that is absolutely and cruelly real. The power of it is indescribable, as vital on the first step as it is on the last, at the base or on the summit, and the intensity only gradually fades on your return to the valley.

Climbers don't want anything different. They want excitement, like everyone, and fear death, like everyone. But the fear doesn't inhibit the desire. Instead there is a special addictive thrill that comes from keeping the fear suppressed. The analogy with violence is obvious. To imagine yourself becoming a violent person you have to imagine your inhibitions at assaulting others not just melting away, but being forced down out of sight, and then finding that doing this gives you a satisfied and elated feeling, the absence of which you will later miss.

SELF-IMAGE AND RESPECT FOR OTHERS

We get another glimpse of what it is like to be violent by thinking about self-respect. What kind of a person does a violent individual take himself to be? Although it is a platitude of our society that troubled personalities usually suffer from low self-esteem, the evidence about violent individuals suggests something more subtle. Violent individuals are more likely to have inflated than deflated beliefs about their own capacities and the attitudes of others to them. On the other hand these beliefs are often wildly at variance with the facts. It is not uncommon for violent rapists to believe that they are masters of sexual technique, or for abusive fathers to believe that their children adore them. The self-esteem of these people is based on claims that their behavior contradicts. Their self-esteem is thus both inflated and vulnerable. The profile of the "fragile egotist" is in fact very common among violent individuals. Such people have a need to gather evidence for their inflated and implausible views of themselves, and so they need signs of respect from others. Respect means at the very least deference. In some situations it means fear: someone does not respect you unless they tremble in your presence. And so the violent person has no shortage of occasions on which to explode: to treat her as a normal human being is to mock her true majesty.

We can imagine part of how it is to have such an unstable self-image by seeing a connection with the violentization process. In order to become violent you have to overcome your inhibitions against harming others. This takes willpower in a normal person. You make yourself do it, train yourself into it. But this means that you follow a policy of turning yourself into a violent person: at some level you know what you are doing. Becoming violent, becoming feared, is a target you aim at, so when you reach the target you know what you have done, what you now are. To some extent this is like making yourself unafraid of heights or of handling corpses: you are likely to think of yourself in terms of the person you have allowed yourself to become. And you are proud of the kind of person you have become. But there is a complicating factor in the case of violence. You have allowed yourself to become a person whose nature is not entirely welcome to those around you. It would take a very subtle person to hold both of these sides of the picture accurately in mind at once. A more likely reaction is to hold on to just one of the alternatives, almost invariably the one most favorable to you, and to acknowledge the other only when it is forced on you.

The result is that you embrace something that you know, at least subconsciously, those around you value much less than you do. It is like being an adolescent in a conservative social environment whose social style focuses on offbeat jokes and bizarre sinister art. You have to think of yourself as a jester or a rebel artist, and you have to think of this as a desirable thing to be. But you also know that many of your contemporaries, the people whose opinion matters to you, think you are weird. So you develop a double image: proud possessor of a rare talent and weird deviant. Or it is like being the environmentally conscious exception in a throwaway society. Your fifteen-year-old Toyota is a source of pride when you compare yourself with your neighbors. But you are very vulnerable to slipping unpredictably down into their conception of you, as eccentric, laughable, and no ornament to the neighborhood.

If your sense of your self has different bases than those of others, you will have trouble understanding what counts as respect or humiliation in their eyes. So your dealings with others will be liable to misunderstandings and miscalculations. This will happen with all the ordinary examples I have just given. Violent people, though, are not dangerous just by misunderstanding. They have two further motives for wanting to humiliate others. First there is simply the thrill of suppressing the inhibitions to violence. Then there is the need to bolster an unstable sense of their own value.

We all maintain images of ourselves that are vulnerable to undermining by obvious facts. And we all can find ourselves at an overlap point between two ways of thinking of ourselves, so that, to adapt the image of the previous section, a small change in one's situation can set off an uncomfortable drop down to a much less complimentary sense of one's own value. That is part of the human condition, and it gives us a glimpse of what it is like to have gone through the process that makes an individual violent. Only a glimpse, but in understanding things like this, we should be grateful for every little handle we can give our imagination.

SOCIOPATHS

Violence is not the only way people can be a menace to others. There is also cheating, stealing, and heartbreak. In all of these ways a person can harm another, without the use of physical violence and without inducing fear. But in all of these the potential benefits of harming others are inhibited by, among other things, our reluctance to cause distress. There are people who have much less reluctance to cause distress than the rest of us. These are the sociopaths.

It is important to be clear about the terminology here. A person with many of the characteristics that are now gathered under the label "sociopath" would not long ago have been described by psychologists as a "psychopath." But the concept of a psychopath is a confusing one. On the one hand, the word seems to mean "pathological psyche" and is often used in everyday speech to mean "dangerously crazy person." And on the other hand, even when defined more carefully, it tends to run together what is best called sociopathy with the violent personality types we have been discussing. Moreover, the two types are not only different, they are in some ways opposites.

A sociopath is someone suffering from antisocial personality disorder, which is defined, in the words of the American Psychiatric Association's *Diagnostic and Statistical Manual of Mental Disorders* (1980) as "a repetitive and persistent pattern of behavior in which the basic rights of others or major age-appropriate societal norms or rules are violated. The specific behaviors . . . fall into one of four categories: aggression to people and animals, destruction of property, deceitfulness or theft, or serious violation of rules." The definition makes most sense if we assume that the "societal norms or rules" are not arbitrary conventions but rules protecting fundamental human interests. Later remarks in the *Manual* make it clear that what is meant is a personality disorder that leads individuals to violate conventional morality in specific ways which cause real harm to others. To quote further,

> Persons with this disorder disregard the wishes, rights, or feelings of others. They are frequently deceitful and manipulative . . . Individuals . . . also tend to be consistently and extremely irresponsible. . . . [They] show little remorse for the consequences of their acts. They may be indifferent to, or provide a superficial rationalization for, having hurt, mistreated, or stolen from someone. . . . These individuals may blame the victims for being foolish, helpless, or deserving their fate; they may minimize the harmful consequences of their actions; or they may simply indicate complete indifference.

The picture emerges pretty clearly from these quotes. Sociopaths primarily lack certain emotions: sympathetic pleasure at another's happiness, dismay at another's sorrow, remorse at having brought trouble to another. I shall use this lack of sympathy as my definition of the condition. It should be clear how different from the profile of the violent individual this is. There is no crossing a threshold from normal to pathological: the sociopath is always operating in the same mode, and is incapable of operating any other way. There is no pleasure at harming or humiliating others, simply an indifference when the individual's pursuit of her own ends results in harm or humiliation to another. (Paradoxically, the violent person cares more about her victim than the sociopath.) The image of the violent individual is one of deliberate aggression while that of the sociopath is one of cool calculated manipulation.

Assuming Blair's theory of the processes that inhibit violence, we may put the contrast this way: a violent individual has suppressed or found ways around the inhibitions, while a sociopath has no need to learn to do this, since the inhibitions are already absent. The distress of others that would normally trigger them fails to, so they do not need to be overcome. There are two ways in which this can happen. The distress of others can fail to be recognized as having any special significance, or it can be recognized but fail to trigger an inhibition. These are different. Blair's work tends to emphasize the second, but sociopathy is a symptom and not a disease, and we do not know how varied the causes may be. So, though the numbers must be small, there is the possibility of the gentle sociopath, who has no inclination to violence but also no concern for the effect his actions have on others.

This is not to say that a sociopath is unlikely to be violent. He may have undergone the violentization process; he may have developed an image of himself as a violent person; he may have found a way of life in which violence pays off. But he is violent and also sociopathic, rather than violent because sociopathic. Sociopaths are further removed from the standard form of humanity than violent individuals, although, paradoxically, they often seem more normal than violent people. The reason for this is that from an early age the sociopath has learned to interact with others in a way that mimics sympathy or remorse. An intelligent sociopath will have learned how to seem to have the emotions that mediate human interactions, so that others will interact with him, until at some point, when the stakes are right, this appearance is discarded. An evocative depiction of the sociopathic personality is the film The Grifters (1990), in which a sociopathic mother and son both earn their living by deceiving others. Neither is routinely violent, though both are completely ruthless, and the single act of violence by the mother at the end of the film is unintentional and leaves her bewildered.

Can we imagine what it is like to be a sociopath? Here is a clue. When I describe the sociopathic profile to people, they very often pause for a moment and then describe an ex-spouse or ex-lover – just occasionally a current spouse or lover – as sociopathic. My interpretation of this – unless the world is dotted with sociopaths – is that when one has to detach oneself emotionally from someone, one often is led to denying that the emotions that person had were real. Separation involves a sudden change of perspective that cuts one off from the emotions that were evident when the relationship was live. Many of us have experienced this; and have also been the object of it. So imagine being the kind of person an ex-partner thinks you are. Suppose that in reaction to their new image of you, you decided to live up to it, to be emotionally distant and uncaring while presenting a perfect impression of commitment and compassion. Then you would be imagining yourself as mildly sociopathic. Or, to come at it from a different angle, imagine situations in which you fake the emotions that are required. Your child has fallen and scratched her knee, and after a day of childcare your reserves of sympathy are drained. But you know that a good parent would show sympathy, encouragement, and concern. So you produce as many

On Evil

of the signs of this as you can, although in your heart you just wish the moment would pass and you could get on to the next task. Now imagine that in most of your interactions with people you were faking it in this way: to the extent that you can imagine this, you are imagining part of what it is to be a sociopath.

Sociopaths have no need to humiliate others. They don't care enough to be bothered to. Their image of themselves does not require harm to others. What does it require? It is hard to imagine what a sociopath's sense of self is like, harder than imagining that of a violent individual. We want to know what a sociopath values and tries to develop in himself. But it is hard to know what in such a personality counts as valuing. I think the difficulty is partly one of separating emotions. When imagining sociopathy we tend to imagine complete lack of emotion. But this is not so: satisfaction, joy, disappointment, regret (as opposed to remorse) are all available. But we have trouble imagining this selective failure of emotion.

The psychology of most kinds of dangerous people involves some deficit in the grasp of what it is to be another person. The violent individual has difficulty understanding that people do not rank others favorably in terms of their capacity to inspire fear. The sociopath has difficulty understanding that many human acts are performed either for the sake of the interaction itself or in order to benefit others. One might conjecture that sociopaths have difficulty with tasks that require one to put oneself imaginatively in another person's situation, especially where this situation is an essentially social one. But as far as I know, there are no hard data on this.

It is worth comparing these deficits with those of autistic people. In autism the person has difficulty understanding the beliefs and thoughts of other people, especially false beliefs and thoughts that depart from reality. The autistic person's understanding of speech is very literal. As a result of these difficulties or because of the condition that causes them, the social manner of autistic people is generally withdrawn and impersonal.

Autistic people are no more dangerous than any of the rest of us. If anything they are less of a menace since their capacity for deception is less. The existence of the autistic syndrome, though, warns us to be careful how we characterize sociopathy. It involves a failure of specific aspects of the capacity to grasp what it is to be another person. Exactly what aspects is not easy to say. I mention this just to make the point that a deficit in understanding other people does not make one morally deficient. A particular kind of gap in one's grasp of other people is required.

The deficits of psychopaths in understanding the nature of morality are made explicit in the work of Robert Blair (1995), already referred to. Blair replicated Turiel's experiment, in which small children showed that they could distinguish between violations of convention and violations of basic moral principle, using dangerous prison inmates as subjects. Blair found that these subjects performed significantly less well than small normal children in making the distinction. In effect, they thought of all moral rules as conventional, as social arrangements that one has to stay on the right side of unless one can avoid being caught, but which have no intrinsic force. The evidence suggests that they simply do not grasp the distinction. It was this that led Blair to postulate a VIM.

A philosopher discussing these results, Shaun Nichols (2002), suggests that the explanation is that sociopaths operate in all moral contexts by grasping an articulated set of principles, a "moral theory," which specifies what is socially acceptable in various circumstances. In terms of this, a sociopath can in fact believe that murder and fraud are "wrong." But he won't deduce from this, as someone else might, that he should take the steps to avoid them.

A curious consequence of this view is that a sociopath could in principle be a moral person. Suppose that some sociopath is convinced that it is in her interest to act morally, perhaps for fear of hellfire or because she thinks that others are very good at detecting when she has done wrong. And suppose that she has a comprehensive theory specifying what is right and wrong. Then she has self-interested reasons to act charitably and sympathetically to others, to treat them honestly, and so on. And so she will. How much like real morality will this be? That depends on how much of morality you think could be summed up in a theory. Some philosophers have put a lot of work into trying to formulate such theories. As if they were trying to make life easier for sociopaths! (One might think here of the Nazi Adolf Eichmann, discussed in the next chapter, who thought of himself as a follower of the rule-oriented moral philosophy of Kant.) More recent philosophers have been much more skeptical that the ways we should treat one another can be summed up in any theory that any human being could grasp.

THE BARRIER THEORY OF EVIL

To describe someone as violent or as a sociopath is not to call them or their acts evil. In fact, no purely psychological profile will serve as a definition of evil. But we can guide ourselves towards a definition by connecting the psychology of dangerous people with a philosophical account of motivation, designed to illuminate our judgments of moral character. It is important to be clear, though, that far more evil acts are performed by perfectly normal people out of confusion or desperation or obsession than by violent individuals and sociopaths. What we have to look for are very general similarities between the various different pathological psychologies and the motivation behind more everyday evil. We are looking for the kind of motivation to which our reactions of horror and disgust are attuned.

To state my theory I need to begin with a sketch of the typical pattern of motivation for any act. Consider a person facing a problem. She has locked herself out of her car, for example. The first thing she'll do is to think of possible solutions. She might break the car window; she might go into a nearby store to call a garage; she might walk home and get her spare keys. Then she will evaluate these solutions, looking for advantages and disadvantages. If one or two seem promising she will investigate them further, both in terms of detailed comparisons of pros and cons and in terms of how she might carry them out. If none seems promising, she will try to think of some more solutions. And eventually she will do something. Most of the process will happen so automatically that she will not know it is happening. In particular, she is unlikely to be aware of having selected only a small number of possible actions to think about out of the infinitely many things she could have done. (She could have taken off all her clothes in order to attract the police, who might have been able to get her car open. She could have set fire to the car so that the problem of getting it to its destination disappeared.) And she will normally be completely in the dark about why she considers some actions and not others.

Moral considerations arise explicitly when we compare actions. But they enter invisibly at an earlier stage, when solutions are selected for further consideration. The person locked out of her car does not even consider grabbing a passerby and smashing a car window with his head. The most basic reason is surely not fear of reprisals or of the law, but a deep fact about human beings, that our planning does not readily fasten on acts involving damage or suffering to others. There is a barrier against such options being considered. The barrier is not insuperable. If all the obvious ways of getting into the locked car fail, our person may consider phoning her partner and making him feel so guilty about her having locked herself out that he leaves his work, in spite of the deadline he is up against, and drives home to get the spare keys then out to where she is. But we need to be forced to consider options that would otherwise be filtered out by our inbuilt barriers against harm.

We filter out harmful actions unconsciously. (You'd worry about the sanity of a friend who even considered doing things that resulted in your death or mutilation, even if she always rejected them.) Some tendency to this must be an inbuilt feature of our species, but we must also learn ways of doing it. We filter our options for many reasons. One reason is that a large part of the art of being successful in any domain is thinking of the right things to do, i.e. filtering out the wrong things. And a large part of being a good, responsible participant in social life consists in being able to know, immediately, what the right things to do are. These are the virtues. Aristotle gave us the right picture of them. Courage consists in knowing when it is right to confront a threat and when it is foolish. The brave person makes the right choice in situations in which it would take too long to solve the problem consciously.

So blocking harmful actions is only one reason why we need filters for possible actions. But it is the reason that is important now. The essence of evil motivation is the failure to block actions that ought not even to have been considered. Now some of the actions that even the most virtuous person filters out of consideration would in fact have been beneficial. And some actions that should have been blocked turn out well, so that as reprehensible as the motivation may be, the result is not evil. So a first attempt at a definition would be to say that an evil act is *an act whose foreseeable results involve the suffering or humiliation of others and whose performance should not have been considered.* Evil is what we should have barriers within our own minds against.

Note the "should." The definition is unashamedly value-laden. Note also various fudges and ambiguities. Perhaps there are situations in which one ought to consider bringing death, agony, or humiliation to innocent people. Certainly there are barriers to consideration of acts besides the primal inhibition of violence. As we grow up and learn to be the kinds of people who can function in complex societies, we learn to make decisions that do not impose unreasonable burdens on others, and so we learn ways of filtering our options that bring the cooperative possibilities to the foreground. So many of the barriers that ought to be in place are learned. Breaching these barriers can result in evil, too, as long as they are in fact barriers that ought to be in place.

I called this a first attempt at a definition. It has a couple of problems. It allows any wrongful breach of a barrier against atrocity to count as evil. But this does not seem right. If someone under extreme provocation strikes another, hurting them badly, then the act may be wrong, but does not seem evil. The definition also presents a problem with non-violent or white-collar evil. It is important that there be such a category, that we not reserve the label of evil for things that happen to arouse our immediate revulsion rather than things that on reflection we realize are in the relevant way deeply wrong. But the present definition either includes too much or too little. Almost all of our actions have seriously bad consequences for some other people, somewhere in the world in the fullness of time, and very many of these are actions which we ought to have the moral sense, if only we had the time and intelligence to reflect properly, not even to consider. So the danger in the definition is that if we interpret it too literally, then just about everything anyone does counts as evil, and if we interpret it with provisos for our limited powers of reflection and insight, then it will exclude many cases in which people do evil without realizing it. We need a definition that goes a bit more deeply into patterns of motivation.

The definition I suggest is this. *A person's act is evil when it results from a strategy or learned procedure which allows that person's deliberations over the choice of actions not to be inhibited by barriers against considering harming or humiliating others that ought to have been in place.* An isolated act of anger, then, will not be evil, because it does not result from a process that the person uses regularly. On the other hand the rages of a violent individual will result in evil, because they are an acquired strategy for achieving that person's ends. We shall see that the definition leaves a lot of room for non-violent or unaware evil. This evil will often take the form of a kind of self-deception, where a person, usually with the help of others, finds ways of making herself blind to the awful consequences of her actions.

The emphasis on self-deception links with a very important fact. Our cultures and societies are very imperfect creations, which have developed by many accidental turns of fate in the search for ways in which human beings can live decent lives together. Each actual society depends for its stability on factors that are of dubious moral status. Extreme examples are slave-owning societies or societies depending on the subjugation of women. Nearly all societies have consented to, and probably depended on, controlling children with physical threats, punishments, and constraints. Our society depends on practices of incarcerating criminals, which produce a lot of suffering for often disappointing results, and of dividing the world by national borders, over which most people cannot freely move. It depends on raising millions of animals in bad conditions and then slaughtering them in factories.

No doubt future societies will look back and applaud some aspects of our practices, and for others they will sigh or shudder and wonder why it took people such a long time to see that they were indefensible. But we, in the middle of it all, cannot easily see what is defensible and what is not. In fact, we would not be able to function as members of society if we could. Sometimes we have hints that our society is far from ideal, and usually we manage to shove them away into the back of our minds. Think of the dim awareness that many conventional members of slave-owning societies must have had that their world rested on an evil basis, deriving from moments of sympathy for the suffering of particular slaves, doctrines of the rights of man, or Christian doctrines of the love of God for all people. Such doubts are quickly swept away, but if they occur too often we learn sweeping techniques. We learn strategies for not noticing that our actions lead to atrocity. And then our actions are evil. In this way most decent well-meaning responsible people are complicit in evils of which they are at most dimly aware.

The opposite happens too, for the same reasons. Just as it can become easy to learn ways around our inhibitions against harm, and so do evil, it can be hard to learn acceptable ways around the inhibitions. We learn rules about when harm is permissible, and some of these rules go against our instincts. Suppose that you are protecting a child from a smooth sociopathic pedophile. You have a gun and the predator approaches you, with an innocent smile and his hand held out, ignoring your warnings not to come nearer. "You wouldn't shoot me, would you? Just let me explain what is really going on." You know that if he gets any nearer he will be able to take the gun from you, and then the child. You ought to shoot, though if possible not aim to kill. To do this you will have to overcome your inhibitions against violence. This may be easy or hard, depending on your upbringing and character. Your culture may have equipped you with a stereotype of evil child molesters, which makes it easier for you to harm someone you take to be one. In this case the stereotype has served well, giving you an easier way to the right act. Your act is not evil, because the inhibition ought to have been overcome in this case. We need these culturally defined norms, which neutralize natural sources of sympathy. Without them we would sometimes be prevented from doing what we ought. But they're dangerous. There is no easy way of telling when the rules are really right, and when they are a cultural excuse for evil. In extreme cases, times of horror, people sometimes have to act against what their consciences have learned to tell them. As Hannah Arendt (1963) puts it, "Many Germans . . . probably an overwhelming majority of them, must have been tempted *not* to murder, *not* to rob, *not* to let their neighbors go off to their doom."

SMALL-SCALE EVIL

The definition has some consequences that I find desirable, but which might be controversial. For one thing, it suggests that evil actions need not be motivated by malice. A sociopath, for example, might see that the way to get the new car he wants is to defraud an old couple of their life savings, without having any desire to hurt them. It's just the best means to achieve his ends. It seems to me just obvious that the sociopath's act is as evil as it would be if he had relished the thought of their poverty and despair. The image of the heartless sociopath is useful to keep in mind, as a reminder that we can do evil by indifference as easily as by malice.

Just as malice is not essential, neither is violence. The significant fact about violence is that it produces suffering, and that to act violently we have to overcome barriers that are there for good reason. But there are many ways of producing suffering, and there are many barriers that ought to be there, and many ways of persuading oneself around them. So there is a lot of room for white-collar evil. The corrupt civil servant who approves the construction of an apartment building in an earthquake zone in the knowledge that it will fall down in a serious tremor is doing something evil. The church official who transfers a priest, against whom credible charges of pedophilia have been made, to another task in which he will continue to deal with children, is also acting evilly.

The most controversial consequence of the definition is that it allows small-scale evil, evil acts that do not involve killing, major suffering, or life-destroying humiliation. For sometimes you shouldn't even consider doing something that harms another person, although the harm is comparatively minor. Suppose that I am giving a lecture and a student asks me a question that I don't know the answer to. One way of saving face is to retort: "The fact that you ask that question shows how little you grasp the topic. Does someone have an intelligent question?" This will certainly shut the student up, and it will also produce dismay and possibly depression. It is something that should not even occur to me. Or consider someone who has been entrusted with an extremely embarrassing secret, and tells it to the world. This too has something in common with much more serious evil-doing: it ignores a barrier against the humiliation of others.

So the definition allows some things that are towards the lower edge of what most people would regard as evil. It does this deliberately: I'll say why soon. And it also deliberately excludes many kinds of wrongdoing, including some seriously wrong acts. It will exclude acts, however wrong, that result from incompetence and miscalculation. And it will exclude non-atrocious acts, which are wrong, even very wrong, but which do not involve death, suffering, or humiliation.

Probably most non-evil wrongdoing falls into one of these three categories. An example of the first would be the case of Truman and the atomic bomb, as I described it in chapter one. Examples of the second kind of non-evil wrongdoing, miscalculation, are everywhere. Nearly always when someone tells a lie to get out of a tight spot, or takes something that does not belong to them, the act is wrong but not evil. For the act is not of a kind we are forbidden ever to perform, let alone to consider.

The third kind of non-evil wrongdoing, non-atrocity, is one that we often overlook. It contains injustices, deceptions, and breaches of trust, among other things, with consequences that can be seriously bad, but do not include major damage to particular victims. Suppose that the admissions officer of a law school insinuates gender-sensitive criteria into its policies, so that far fewer women are admitted than would otherwise be. This is unjust, and he should be condemned for it. But it is not evil. The victims are all college graduates who have other ways of earning their living. They may earn less money or have less satisfying lives than if they had not been unjustly treated, but no one of them has her life smashed as a consequence simply of this. The results of the unjust law-school policy may be at least as bad as those of many evil actions, inasmuch as we can compare a medium-sized injustice inflicted on thousands of people to an atrocity inflicted on fewer. But the issue here is not which is worse but which is evil. If the label "evil" is to do any work beyond dramatizing a sense of disapproval, it must be withheld from injustices that do not bring pain, death, or humiliation to particular people.

REAL EVIL

There is a point to defining evil as I did, with the result that many terribly wrong acts are excluded, and some less than terribly wrong acts are at least borderline cases. The point is to focus on something deeper than what happens to arouse immediate horror in us, and more specific than what is generally wrong. I am looking for a concept with explanatory force and moral importance, so that, in characterizing an action as evil, one is saying something about why it happened and about how we should react to it. The barrier theory of evil does this. Evil acts arise from a specific failure of the way we choose our actions, in which the barriers against atrocity are overcome or eroded. Of course, there are many ways in which this can happen, and some of them are important enough to deserve being studied in their own right. In particular, understanding the various systematic forms of the self-deception, by which we persuade ourselves that our harmful acts are really OK, would be of enormous value. And it is important to understand better the processes by which a normal child becomes a violent adult. But these and other forms of evil motivation have enough in common that it says something significant about an act to characterize it as evil.

A comparison with courage may be helpful. Courageous acts are produced for many different reasons, by many different kinds of people. They result from a specific motivational trait, which results in the person taking large but not insane amounts of risk to accomplish valuable ends. (This is the non-trivial concept of courage, which excludes foolhardiness.) This trait works differently in someone who shows, say, the intellectual courage to defend an unpopular view, from someone who goes into a collapsing office building to save workers trying to get out. Someone could have the one courage but not the other. Whatever kind of courage someone has, though, it will lead them to do courageous things, and often the understanding this gives us of their actions cannot be got in any other way. Suppose that you want to know what someone with political courage will do in a situation in which he is being attacked for holding a generally unpopular view. Will he pretend that he does not really subscribe to that exact position, or will he try to persuade the public that his view, though currently unpopular, is right? The second course might be the courageous one, but it also might be political suicide. To know what he might do and what he definitely will not do, you have to know what the courageous options are. You have to be able to understand or imagine how a courageous person thinks. There's no substitute; if you don't understand courage then you can't do it.

Similarly, if you want to know what an evil person will do, you have to have some understanding of evil. Understanding moral incompetence, weakness of will, irresponsibility, and other forms of bad character, will not help. It is evil you need. Suppose you are doing business with a very intelligent, very self-righteous and moralistic, but evil tycoon. You know that he will find some way to deprive you of a lot of money, which will be both ingeniously hard to resist and also defensible according to some thought-out and superficially plausible principles. That is what you have to be prepared for; since he is evil he will have a way around the obstacles to hurting you, and since he is a moralistic financial genius this is the kind of way he will find. Knowing that he was just a *bad* financial genius would not give you anything like this information. So what calling an act or a person evil does is to tell you to look for a certain way of choosing acts, one that will not be blocked by barriers to harm. What way you find will depend on what kind of evil it is, and what kind of person.

Evil acts, understanding them my way, will have a lot in common with acts that are not seriously wrong enough to get classed as evil, but which have the same sort of psychological and moral character. I discussed these in the previous section. They will also have a lot in common with some acts that are very serious – they have atrocious consequences – but are not evil because they are not wrong. I am thinking of acts of justified harm. The simple examples are like the example above of having to shoot someone to protect a child. But there are harder cases. There are people whose motivation would lead to evil acts were they in other circumstances but who by moral luck find themselves living lives in which their tendencies to harm work to the good. The obvious example is war, when to defend your country against attack you have to kill the attackers. Come peacetime, some genuine war heroes will find that the same tendencies that made them indispensable in resisting evil now put them in danger of committing evil themselves.

Of course, the "good atrocities" can really be just plain evil. It is notoriously hard to tell, and the self-doubt of killers and torturers in a supposedly good cause is a frequent theme in fiction and film. From the "grand inquisitor" section of Dostoevsky's *The Brothers Karamazov* (which tells a fable in which Christ returns and is condemned by the Inquisition) to Ridley Scott's film *Blade Runner* (in which a destroyer of sentient androids realizes that they are sentient as well as androids) to *The Quiet American* (both Graham Greene's novel and the two film versions, whose theme is "I never knew a man who had better motives for all the trouble he caused") authors have probed the ambiguities of situations in which an apparently good cause requires someone to violate the prohibitions against doing awful things to others. Someone trying to understand the actions of someone operating in this morally intermediate zone will have to operate very nearly – but not exactly! – as if they were understanding the motivation behind evil actions.

EVIL PEOPLE, EVIL SOCIETIES

I slipped just now into talking about evil people. But the barrier theory is a theory of evil acts. It is important to keep the acts and the people separate, since anyone can do an evil act, and most of the actions of even the most awful people are not at all evil. The simplest slide from acts to people is to call someone evil when they produce a lot of evil acts. There's a deeper connection, though. According to the barrier theory, an evil act results from a systematic way of traversing the barriers against atrocity. This can come from fundamental features of people's personalities: the way they select actions, or the way they deceive themselves. So it makes more sense to think of an evil person as one whose personality has as a central element some way of negotiating the barriers.

There are four obvious kinds of evil personalities. There are people who just do not have the normal barriers against atrocity. The extreme example might be a violent sociopath, the kind of person once called a psychopath. Then there are people who have undergone a process that has taught them ways around the barriers, that they can activate when needed. The model is violentization. The third kind is people who have acquired beliefs from their cultures which neutralize the barriers. The prime examples are ethnic prejudices and moral beliefs which too easily give permission for atrocity. And the fourth kind is people who invent for themselves beliefs and ways of thinking that facilitate transgression. Dangerous fantasies of one's own superiority, or self-created ideology, will do the job here.

In the second and third of these a person has become evil with the help of her society. That's the real temptation, the vampire outside the window, in respectable clothing with a warm and encouraging face. We all absorb from our societies permissions to do or allow evils to happen to others. And some, many, of these permissions are as they should be, to the extent that each society depends on some tendency to atrocity, and could not easily change to avoid this. But we just take them all for granted, we hardly notice them, and so we rarely bother to reflect on which ones are sad-but-necessary and which ones make us accomplices.

Because it is so hard to reflect intelligently on these things, people in one society can be quite unable to grasp how they are seen by people in another. An important example is the complementary images of members of comfortable and desperate societies. Take a rich and stable society in interaction with a poor and troubled one. The United States and Central America; Israel and Palestine; in fact this is now the global norm, comfortable and desperate economically entwined however far apart they may be socially and geographically. The rich society cannot see why people in the poor one do not simply act as the rich do and live lives like theirs. They suspect the poor of wanting their goods without having to work for them, and thus think of them as potential thieves, who would not hesitate to do violence to a rich person. They see the whole poorer society in terms of the image of a violent individual.

The poorer society, on the other hand, cannot see why people in the rich society do not help them, in ways that would cost them very little. They suspect the rich of indifference to the plight of anyone who is not like them. They suspect that it simply does not bother the rich what the lives of the poor are like, because they are incapable of imagining them with any sympathy. They see the whole richer society through the image of a sociopath.

The two images feed on one another. Consider the 9/11 hijackers. They saw themselves as attacking a powerfully evil enemy, so powerful that pity for its members would be misplaced. (To get the mentality, think of the emotions the audience has in empathizing with the rebels in the first *Star Wars* film as they attack the death star. It is a brooding dark fortress of evil, and when it is blown up the audience hardly notices that thousands of its inhabitants have died.) The 9/11 hijackers were moved on an ideological level by hatred of western culture and in particularly America. That is not enough to motivate their actions, though. After all, this hatred was linked to loyalty to Islam, which explicitly prohibits targeting non-combatants in war. Many of them were moved by a fascination with martyrdom. At least one of them, Mohammed Atta, the dominant personality in the group, had a deep hatred of women. In fact the people who had considered Atta a potential menace in the months before were all women. We shall never know the exact combination of emotions and beliefs involved, but they must have included ways of keeping out of mind the humanity of the people they would kill. Their image of America as evil − as a coldly calculating sociopathic menace to what they held valuable − was intrinsic to their capacity to do this.

To its credit, American society has to a large extent avoided the opposite temptation, to see all the varied Islamic cultures through the image of the violent individual. But this tolerance should not prevent us asking the essential question of any society: what resources does it offer individuals for blinding themselves to what they are doing to others? That is part of what we have to understand about any perpetrator: what ways of getting around the barriers to atrocity were working here? Take that, in fact, as the central message of this book. Don't ask just about evil desires; look more deeply, at the failures of the barriers that should prevent some desires being acted on.

Three

This chapter is about the real horrors, the real nightmare figures. It is about our nightmares as well as the reality. It asks how our images of the worst kinds of people relate to the people themselves, and whether the images sustain and shape the realities. One aim of the chapter is to understand better what the difficulties are in imagining what it is like to be a person who does the things these people do.

Terrorists, serial killers, rapists, tyrants and their accomplices: torturers, secret police, concentration camp guards. Bin Laden, Bundy, Sutcliffe, Hitler, Eichmann, Stalin, Beria. These are the people we most hope to avoid. But they are all very different. It is extremely hard to imagine being a serial killer, at least someone fitting the standard profile of a serial killer. Though you may doubt this, it is not too hard to imagine being a terrorist or to see how you might become one. I try to overcome your doubt later in the chapter. The accomplices of tyrants are midway in imaginability. Hannah Arendt's thesis of the banality of evil is meant to apply to such people. If it is right, then they are less different from the rest of us than we like to think, and the differences are not the ones we might suppose. I shall agree with much of what Arendt says about agents of atrocious regimes, and disagree with its significance for other kinds of evil. In any case, it is important to see how different all these horrors are. So I shall deal with them one by one. I will not deal with every nightmare image. I have thought and read about only so many, and I do not think I could bear to learn too much more. I shall discuss serial killers, then the agents of state-sponsored atrocity, and then the depiction of killers in fiction.

SERIAL KILLERS

There certainly are people who kill numbers of victims, one by one over a period of time, not for money or any obvious gain. Some time in the second half of the twentieth century the existence of serial killers became widely known, and a fascination developed in literature and film. A list of real killers is known to many of us. Ted Bundy, with his suave and persuasive manner that could overcome intelligent women's reservations about accompanying a strange man to an unknown destination. Jeffrey Dahmer, with his refrigerator filled with parts of the men he had drugged, killed, and raped, sometimes after their deaths. Harold Shipman, the doctor whose elderly female patients died, one after another. Fred and Rosemary West, from whose house many girls never reappeared. With the fascination came an image of the serial killer as driven by incomprehensible motives, but also extremely clever and devious at finding victims and evading detection. Crazy but also clever. It seems beyond doubt that even without the media fascination there would be serial killers, though they wouldn't have that label to apply to themselves and possibly to be influenced by. It seems likely, also, that there have always been serial killers, as a very small proportion of the population, and that they have always been responsible for a very small proportion of violent deaths.

There is a profile of a serial killer's crimes that fits a large number of cases. The killer usually specializes in killing people of the gender of his sexual preference. More often than not the killer is a man, so the victims are usually either women or gay men. Prostitutes are favorite targets. One reason is simply that prostitutes are available and vulnerable. But the targets are very varied.

Behind these patterns there are the minds of the killers. There is a pattern here too, though also many exceptions to each element. Sometimes, far from always, there is a childhood history of physical or sexual abuse. The killer is very often socially isolated and withdrawn in adolescence. Fantasies of violence, often with a sexual content, are frequent in adolescence and early adulthood. The tendency to fantasy is often accompanied by an emotional flatness: in normal life the killer often does not feel very much. There is sometimes a tendency to obsessiveness and to obsessive collecting. At some point the first killing happens, often almost by accident. There is often then a gap before the next. But, perhaps after one or more further gaps, a series of killings follow, which can continue for a long time.

When they are apprehended, serial killers sometimes describe their motives to journalists and criminal psychologists. What they say has to be taken with extreme caution. For one thing they are being asked about levels of motivation where everyone's self-knowledge is very unreliable. No one can say with any authority why they have the sexual preferences they do, or why they have chosen the style of life they have. Killers have a better chance of knowing how they planned their crimes, and what thoughts and feelings went through their minds at the time, but there's a big gap between saying what they thought and felt and saying why. Even on the topic of "what," we should treat what they say with caution. Like everyone else, they are trying to make their lives fit into an intelligible pattern, but they are confined to the assumptions and vocabulary that people use to describe more normal lives, which may be very misleading when applied to them. And they are trying to make their lives seem meaningful, even fascinating, rather than squalid and revolting. Thus Bundy, who had a degree in abnormal psychology and was in good command of a sophisticated vocabulary to confuse others and himself, claimed that his motive was simply rape, and that the killings were incidental. And Joel Rifkin, who killed seventeen young women in the New York area in the 1980s, claimed to have had no interest in necrophilia, though the physical evidence seems to contradict this. We should not credit these people with much self-knowledge.

So what is going on in the head of a serial killer? The individuals vary greatly, and there may be no single psychological pattern behind the cases that evoke the standard cultural image. So you should treat a profile like the one I am about to present with caution. As much caution, perhaps, as the reports of the killers themselves. But imagine the following. A person has a tendency to obsessive thoughts and a fascination with violence. He may not often act violently, but when thoughts of harming others occur to him, especially when combined with sexual fantasy, they persist and go round and round in his head. These are not the only thoughts that go obsessively round in his head. He also tends to have chains of both self-degrading and grandiose thoughts filling his mind uninvited. The self-degrading thoughts are often accompanied by feelings of painful depression.

Then at some point for some reason he kills someone, most likely on impulse in a sexually charged atmosphere, and is lucky enough not to be caught. Although he is horrified at what he has done, he also has an elated and relaxed feeling from letting down the barriers against fantasies that have long been with him. He feels less depressed, more alive. But the barriers now become more strongly policed, since he knows what they can lead to. Then when he is feeling very low again he kills again, and learns that he is addicted to the feeling of release that it gives. He is now dependent on killing for his mental balance.

Call this the K-profile. Some, perhaps many, serial killers will fit at least some aspects of it. And many serial killers certainly will not. The point of presenting the K-profile is not to make a claim about killer psychology but to demonstrate that one can describe in commonsense intuitive terms a mentality that can be responsible for serial killings. This should give some support to the idea that perpetrators of the most awful acts are not completely beyond our powers of intuitive understanding. The K-profile in some ways resembles that of the violent individuals discussed in chapter two. Here too we have a first occasion after which the individual discovers how to overcome barriers against certain acts. But in the K-profile, overcoming the barrier leads to a release that is addictive. The person comes to need it. The profile is also in some ways like that of a sociopath. But people can fit the K-profile without being more than marginally sociopathic, they need not be incapable of sympathizing with others in all contexts. That is one reason why they tend to focus on one category of victims, who by being objects in violent fantasies have ceased to be seen as real people. The K-profile also resembles that of the compulsive gambler or risk-taker.

The sexual aspect of the profile doesn't depend on any intrinsic link between sex and violence. There probably *are* such links, reluctant as we are to admit it. But it would be enough to support this aspect of the K-profile that sexual fantasies have lives of their own, out of the control of the people who have them, so that when they become associated with violent imagery or impulses, these too become haunting and uncontrollable. For people with a tendency to obsessional thinking and violent impulses, the presence of violent pornography featuring the degrading of sexual objects – as opposed to other sexually explicit material – is likely to produce very dangerous connections.

INSANITY?

Are these people insane? The argument for is easy to make, and is routinely made by defense lawyers pleading that their clients are mentally ill and thus should be treated rather than punished. Serial killers do things that risk their lives and their freedom, and their sense of their own human value, for the sake of a sense of release and sexual gratification that could more safely be got from pornography. Is this not irrational in a way that raises doubts about these people's grasp of reality? And their acts are so horrendous. How could a sane person do such things?

The case against is also clear, and is routinely made by prosecution lawyers and their expert witnesses. By definition a serial killer has got away with his crimes on several occasions. This means careful plotting and practical thinking. It often means dealing with other people in a plausible and persuasive manner. Paranoid schizophrenics, in contrast, also commit murders but they rarely get away with more than one, because their inability to function in the practical world makes them very bad at hiding what they have done. And although some serial killers have schizoid symptoms, these are not so severe as to prevent their functioning in the world.

The problem is partly one of words. "Insanity" can mean many things. In a legal context it usually takes on a fairly restricted meaning. In order to be sane enough to be criminally responsible, one has to be capable of understanding the nature of the act one has performed and of appreciating whether it was right or wrong. "Right or wrong" means primarily "legal or illegal" and then secondarily "consistent or inconsistent with the moral ideas of one's society." A sociopath can know the difference between right and wrong on this definition, as long as she understands what is morally required of her, whether or not these requirements activate any inner sense of obligation. These are points frequently made by expert witnesses for the prosecution, in arguing that individuals who have committed crimes that we might think no sane person could contemplate are for all that not insane in the relevant sense. These experts are not denying that the individuals may be mentally ill in some wider sense. They do not function mentally in a way that is likely to lead to decent relations with other people and a satisfying life. But this wider sense of mental illness is quite compatible with criminal responsibility.

There are facts to guide us here, but they do not mesh very well with the questions we are asking. Any answer will have to be laden with care about what we mean by the crucial words "insanity," "responsibility," "blame," "know." Three things are fairly clear.

First, the prosecution experts are right, in that many people who have committed atrocious crimes understand what the rules of society are. They know what will be generally considered to be wrong.

Second, knowledge of right and wrong is a many-sided thing. A sociopath can understand that an act is wrong, in that people forbid and condemn it, while having a very inadequate sense of what is meant by right and wrong. She may have no grasp of the abhorrence wrongdoing arouses in others, especially wrongdoing that involves physical harm. Children, too, have a knowledge of right and wrong that is real but incomplete. As Gitta Sereny says, in discussing the case of the child murderer Mary Bell, "children below twelve years of age do not necessarily have the same understanding as adults of good and bad, of truth and untruths, and certainly of death. . . . even if they really don't know the degree of the wrong they have done, *they always know that they have done wrong*." Such careful formulations are essential if we are to speak seriously of knowledge of right and wrong.

Third, sanity is also a many-sided thing. Most violent criminals, even most serial killers, share most normal desires. And most sane people have more desires to do wrong than they admit. (There is evidence, for example, that most normal men have violent fantasies.) The difference is not so much in what is wanted as what desires are acted upon.

Beyond this point everything is controversial. I shall just state some of my convictions. I am not claiming to have shown that they are true.

We can ask who should be punished. This is in part a practical and legal matter. What does the law actually say? What is it in the interests of society for the law to say? What we want the law to say will depend in part on the attitudes we take to violent criminals. If we regard them as inhuman beasts, then we are blocked from blaming them, any more than one could blame a crocodile, but we are also less compelled to attribute human rights to them. If we regard them as sinners, people like the rest of us but who have done awful things, then blame is straightforward, but we are constrained in how we can treat them. Most violent criminals are neither crocodiles nor simple sinners, but occupy points in a very confusing territory between these extremes.

We shouldn't get too hung up on blame, I think. We should take it that someone is at fault when they knew what would follow from their actions. We should do this even in cases where there are many extenuating circumstances. An example is the child soldiers of many third-world wars. For example, children were kidnapped into the "God's army" in Burma in the 1990s, brutalized, and turned into vicious agents of death and mutilation. The Burmese army itself press-ganged many children. A report of Human Rights Watch describes how a 13-year-old "saw members of his unit massacre 15 Shan minority women and children. . . . after blindfolding and machine-gunning the women, soldiers killed three babies by swinging them by their legs against rocks." Many similar stories come from recent African wars. We should not let our knowledge of how little power these children had to resist what they were being turned into prevent us from saying that each one of them is, tragically, responsible for many crimes.

How we react to blame, on the other hand, should be a much more complex business. Given that someone is responsible for an atrocity, we can react with rage, horror, despair, and many other emotions. To return to the case of children who have killed, we can acknowledge their guilt without falling into the orgy of retributive rage that, for example, engulfed British public opinion towards the two children who killed James Bulger, a todder, in 1993. The British government responded to public opinion by increasing their sentences from eight to fifteen years. The sense that this amounted to playing politics with the children's lives was supported by a ruling of the European Court of Human Rights that they should not have been tried in an adult court. (Or we might decide that a retributive attitude was appropriate: but not without a lot of thought, not as an automatic consequence of responsibility.) In the following chapter of this book I begin to explore the variety of emotions we can have in reaction to evil. There are many of them, and we should think hard and sensitively about which ones make most sense in which cases.

STATE ATROCITY

Two things came together in the twentieth century with horrifying results: the organization of the modern state and pseudo-scientific, quasi-religious ideology. In the name of such ideology, millions were killed in Nazi Germany and the lands it controlled under Hitler, and in the Soviet Union under Stalin. There is nothing new about massacre; humans have been massacring one another since ancient times, often with an intent to exterminate whole populations. And often massacres have been driven by ideology, if we count religious prophecies and enthusiasms. For example the crusades, in the eleventh to thirteenth centuries, were frequently associated with massacres. The first crusade massacred many Jews in Europe, and later crusades massacred many Christians and Muslims in the Near East. The twentieth-century development was the fusion of this ancient tradition with modern communications and the capacity of the modern state to connect with every facet of life.

Most who write about the Holocaust and the Soviet exterminations take for granted that the nature of the states was essential. They were "totalitarian": immense life-and-death power was in the hands of a few unelected leaders who were not accountable to those whose lives they controlled, and right and wrong was defined in terms of a single unquestionable set of beliefs as interpreted by these leaders. It is clear why a totalitarian state has immense resources for evil. It is almost impossible for anyone inside it to challenge its decisions. It is not completely clear that only a totalitarian state can find its way to atrocity. It would be comforting if it were so, especially now that the power in the world is largely in the hands of democracies, imperfect though they may be. All the more reason to be cautious. Could a democracy such as the United States, Britain, or Israel commit large-scale massacres in any way comparable to those committed by the Nazis or the Soviets? I shall return to this question.

The cast of characters in a large-scale, government-instigated atrocity has to be large. The blunt end of the process consists of murders, rapes, tortures, and so there have to be people willing to take part in these. At least some of these people are going to be violent individuals, sadists, and potential serial killers, for example fitting the K-profile above. They must have impulses and fantasies that are satisfied by the atrocities they are asked to commit. They need to be organized and controlled, though, and here people with an ability to restrain violent impulses and fit them into effective overall plans are required. This second class of people, the organizers, do not need to be violent. They can even be repelled by the acts they are organizing. They can be like managers of meat-packing companies who would be nauseated if they ever visited a slaughter-house. But it needs more than an efficient mind. If the organizer is not excited by violence she has to protect herself from it, lest she be appalled. There are two ways of doing this. The first is ideology. If the organizer can persuade herself of the nobility of the overall purpose, then she can steel herself to put up with horrors. Hannah Arendt, in *Eichmann in Jerusalem* (1963), which is the basic and essential reading on this topic, describes the revulsion-appeasing techniques of SS officers, who were generally well educated and intelligent. As she puts it, "Instead of saying: What horrible things I did to people!, the murderers would be able to say: What horrible things I had to watch in the pursuance of my duties, how heavily the task weighed upon my shoulders!"

The other way of keeping revulsion at bay is to have no imagination. This is Arendt's main theme. Her portrait of Adolf Eichmann, the German officer who organized the transportation of Jews from around Europe to extermination camps, is of someone with almost no capacity to think outside fixed practical frames, little capacity to express himself except in clichés and bureaucratese, and minimal capacity to imagine how others might see his acts. It is not a picture of a violent or sadistic man, and in fact Eichmann was horrified on the occasions when he was present during executions. But it is a sense of a man whose lack of imagination is compensated for by an exaggerated sense of duty and obedience. His main pride is on having done a good job, in accordance with the rules as laid down. He thought of himself as a moral man, describing himself as a Kantian, in reference to the German philosopher Kant, who saw morality as a system of rules that everyone must follow. Arendt summed up her shock in discovering that a key player in the Holocaust was not a traditional monster, but simply a very deficient human being, by saying that she had learned of the banality of evil.

Arendt's banality thesis is sometimes taken to be an account of the nature of evil. Evil consists of ordinary people acting in ordinary, unimaginative ways. I read Arendt in a more restricted way, as saying simply: evil can come about this way too. And I suspect Arendt, for all her determination to avoid cultural clichés about evil, of falling into the trap of thinking that similarity of desire means similarity of motivation. She doesn't see that someone can be very abnormal while wanting normal things. The Italian writer Primo Levi, writing about his experiences at Auschwitz, explicitly endorses Arendt's picture, saying, "These were not monsters. I didn't see a single monster in my time in the camp. Instead I saw people like you and I who were acting that way because there was Fascism, Nazism in Germany." Gitta Sereny's picture of Franz Stengl, the commandant of the Treblinka camp, based on many interviews with him, is very similar to Arendt's picture of Eichmann.

But organizers, especially organizers with deficient imaginations, need to be told what direction to organize towards. This is where the third essential category comes in, the ideologues. An ideology is a set of political, economic, social, or religious ideas, which are capable of being interpreted so as to govern most decisions a society has to make. Someone has to interpret them, and to ban heretical or rival ideologies. So we need people interested in controlling a society by a monopoly on the ruling ideas. Their sincerity can vary, from complete sincere faith in a religious dogma to opportunistic fakery. Not all ideologies need lead to large-scale atrocity. An Islamic theocracy, for example, in which a small number of Imams decide basic political questions by reference to their interpretation of the Koran, is not inherently atrocious. Yet the power to suppress dissent is always likely to be used clumsily, and the treatment of people of the Baha'i faith in the only current Islamic theocracy, Iran, is not a good sign. A monopoly of official belief is always likely to attract an alliance with the organizers and the thugs.

The essential feature that allows the atrocities of a totalitarian system is the subservience of the individual conscience to the ideology of the state. In fact "conscience" becomes a rather twisted concept. The truly conscientious, those with the training and willpower that in a civilized society allow people to resist the temptation to harm or take advantage of others, will apply those same qualities to resisting the temptation to behave decently. To repeat Arendt's formulation of it, "Many Germans and many Nazis, probably an overwhelming majority of them, must have been tempted *not* to murder, *not* to rob, *not* to let their neighbors go off to their doom. . . . But, God knows, they had learned how to resist temptation."

Is a totalitarian state required for this inverted kind of conscience? It seems to me doubtful. Large-scale genocidal massacres have occurred in the absence of a powerful state dominating people's lives: Pol Pot's massacres in Cambodia and the massacre of Tutsis in Rwanda. In both of these cases ideology, efficiency, and viciousness all played a role, but without the full trappings of a totalitarian state. A simple despotism can sometimes be as bad. This pushes us towards the question I asked at the beginning of this section. Could a democratic state find itself perpetrating large-scale massacre?

I think the answer is Yes, in spite of the obvious barriers to mass atrocity in democratic societies. Here are two scenarios. In the first a rich democratic society is surrounded by starving neighbors. To prevent catastrophic starvation among its neighbors the rich society would have to devote a large proportion of its domestic product to the purpose. There would then be hardships and shortages. But the people are in the grip of beliefs, according to which giving aid creates dependence that creates more future starvation. The only remedy for poverty, they believe, is self-reliance. So no help is given.

Millions starve. Many in the rich society find the situation unbearable, and manage to prevent themselves from campaigning against the policy of non-intervention only by repeating to themselves the mantra "aid only makes it worse." All schools have to teach the theory of beneficial non-intervention: interventionists are described as being as bad as murderers, since they want to take away the only escape route for the poor. Graphic television coverage of the famines is banned. A century later, when millions have starved, people in the rich society look back in horror at the countless agonizing deaths they were responsible for.

Second scenario. A democratic state suffers a series of terrorist attacks. Suicide bombings, car-bombs, poisoned water supplies, the usual. The blame for the attacks is widely attributed to members of some ethnic minority, with ties to some foreign country. There is some doubt whether this is a complete account of all the atrocities, but a party campaigning on this assumption wins power, democratically, and maintains its power in part by fostering an atmosphere in which adherence to this explanation is part of what makes someone a good and respectable member of society. The attacks continue. Very stringent restrictions are put on the freedom of movement of people in the minority, or people with ties to the foreign country. The attacks continue. Finally the inevitable suggestion is made: all this would end if there were none of these people. A case of vigilante violence against members of the minority leads to a high court decision that members of hostile minorities do not have the protection of the law. Semi-official massacres follow. Later it becomes evident that the vast majority of those massacred were as appalled by the terrorism – at least before the massacres began – as anyone else.

Neither of these scenarios is based on history; perhaps neither is even likely. But they are easily conceivable, and they involve the same ingredients as in other state-sponsored atrocities. They involve ideas that allow people to overcome their revulsion at seeing awful things happen to other people. They involve people who are professionally committed to these ideas, people who organize their application to victims, and a very small number of violent or sadistic individuals. The role of this last group of people, the monsters, is comparatively small. Most of the work is done by ordinary people with every reason to believe that they are responsible and conscientious members of society. Even in a democracy the moral imagination of decent people can be stunted by slogans, labels, and beliefs. It would be an awful irony if the most significant instance of Hannah Arendt's evil banality were found not in the totalitarian situation that led to her reflections, but in the world of individual rights and free elections.

TERRORISTS

Terrorism is the infliction of atrocity for persuasive ends. Terrorism is not war in that the terrorist has no hope of military victory over an opposing force. Instead, the hope is that the reactions of fear, outrage, and demoralization in the enemy society will lead it to concede the terrorists' demands. Defined this way, terrorism does not include acts committed as part of a strategy to win a conventional war. The terror bombings of cities by both sides in the Second World War, designed to break the morale of the opposing population as a means to a military victory, though morally similar to terrorism, or the current "shock and awe" techniques, which aim to undermine morale without many civilian casualties, are not what I am discussing. The terrorist, as I am conceiving of her, is someone whose lack of power gives her little chance of imposing her will on the other by the direct use of force. Her hope of winning is to make the cost of the victory that the other side could obtain if it wanted higher than it can bear.

The terrorist has to inflict atrocities. Unless a sense of horror spreads through the other side, her actions are pointless. Sometimes – if not as often as governments suppose – one can defend a war as the unambiguously right thing to do. But terrorism can never be given this kind of defense, for it always means inflicting the kind of outcome that no human should ever inflict on another. That does not mean that terrorists cannot defend their acts. Their defense has to be of a different kind. They have to describe themselves as being in a moral dilemma, a situation in which there are serious objections to all the available actions. The outline of the terrorist's dilemma is: abandon a just cause or pursue it in the only way available, which has awful consequences. A morally aware terrorist would have to be prepared to take on the guilt of having done something which violates a basic constraint, justified only by the fact that the alternative actions were also unacceptable.

Terrorism entered modern life with the anarchist bombings in the last years of the nineteenth century. The anarchists believed that all governments were instruments of oppression and must be brought down. This kind of anarchism faded away in the twentieth century. The closest analog to anarchist terrorism in contemporary life is the extreme libertarian and white supremacist movements in the US, whose distrust of the federal government combined with lack of real power pushes them to bloody gestures like the bombing of the federal building in Oklahoma City.

The campaigns by weak or minority groups to break up powerful countries so that they can have their own states have been a pervasive form of terrorism in recent history. The IRA in Northern Ireland, the Tamil Tigers in Sri Lanka, ETA in the Basque regions of Spain, Hamas and other groups in the territories occupied by Israel. Each of these has caused a large number of deaths, and induced uncertainty and despair in a large population, by shootings and bombings aimed at any manifestation of a normal civic life in the state they oppose. None of these organizations had a chance of success by direct military confrontation with that state, and so each chose the path of terror instead. None of them has succeeded in winning the concessions it wants, though each has caused considerable disruption and has brought attention to its cause. Each has survived longer than any simple armed uprising would have, and each has provoked the target state into oppressive measures that increase its support among its own group.

A new form of terrorism is now emerging: global terrorism. Here the terrorist group is not campaigning within a country for changes in its internal arrangements but campaigning against a country to produce changes in its policies towards the rest of the world. The dominant form of global terrorism is Islamic. The primary targets are Israel and the United States, and the aim is to produce justice for Palestinians and a relationship between the US and the Islamic world that is – from a fundamentalist point of view – respectful of Islam. The destruction of the World Trade Center on September 11, 2001 turned Islamic global terrorism from a minor irritant into a major factor in American and international life. As a result every society on earth now takes the possibility of various kinds of global terrorism as a fact of life.

The WTC attack was a suicide bombing. The perpetrators knew that they would die, and that if they succeeded they would also cause the death of many innocent people. Suicide bombings are now part of the standard repertoire of terrorism. This should not be surprising. Terrorism is the weapon of those who have strong convictions but little power. Enough conviction to die for one's cause can give a power that is hard for the opponent to match, because the opponent's convictions may be less passionate, and because the opponent is a modern state, based on the idea that violence is taken out of the hands of ordinary citizens and given exclusively to paid agents of the state, who for the most part are just doing a job rather than supporting a cause. The real horror of suicide bombing, though, is that it allows the bomber to get really close to the victims, to act as one of them until the fatal moment. Once there are suicide bombers paranoia takes hold: no one knows when they may be blown up, or by whom.

Most of us would not consider setting off a bomb in a crowded restaurant, let alone walking into a restaurant to blow ourselves up together with the other diners. This would not be among the means we would for a moment consider. We may consider suicide bombers and other terrorists as different beings, as different from us as serial killers. That is a mistake. Among terrorists there are no doubt sadists and potential serial killers. But that mentality is not required for terrorism. In fact, I am sure that most of us can imagine situations in which we would at least consider supporting terrorist acts. Our imagination is blocked by the fact that those situations are so unlike our normal lives.

Imagine that you live in an America that has been taken over by some sinister but very powerful force. Think of it as the Mafia, or as a cartel of international drug dealers. They allow a puppet president and a puppet congress, but no one is nominated for election without Their permission. In the early days a few elected officials spoke and voted against Them but these brave people simply disappeared. Most citizens simply accept the situation and get on with their lives, even though they see a country blighted by corruption, ravaged with drugs, and depressed at being yet another failed experiment in democracy. A few of us, however, gather in small secret groups and talk about what to do. What can we do? We cannot win elections. We cannot start a public debate. We cannot stage demonstrations. To remove Them from power we will have to provoke an absolutely massive uprising. But most people have given up. We have to change the comparative costs, by making the status quo much less acceptable. And that is within our reach. We can assassinate, provoking indiscriminate mass reprisals. We can make complacent public life a nightmare, with bombs and amateur biological weapons. We can bring air travel to a standstill. And all of these will be much easier to accomplish if some of us are willing to die while accomplishing them.

When you imagine this situation, you may know that you would be one of the people who didn't get involved, or who met to complain but advocated non-violence. But you could understand the people who went further than that. So, to that extent, you can imagine being a terrorist, of the most dangerous and appalling kind.

The situation does not fit that of actual terrorism, you may argue. In Northern Ireland or the Basque country there are free elections and a free press. The United States does not control opinions and politics in Islamic countries. These are true observations, but they miss the point. First, many who support terrorism think that their situation is like that in the story, whether or not it really is. Second, democracies often fail to do justice to the aspirations of minority groups, so that the scope for political action can be very restricted. Third, many terrorists live in countries where democratic rights and rights of expression are severely restricted, by governments that they can easily believe, sometimes with evidence, are encouraged by countries that are the objects of their terrorism. And fourth, most basic of all: I was not claiming that you could imagine being, for example, a Palestinian suicide bomber on your way to blow up a restaurant in Jerusalem. To imagine that, you would have to take on a whole culture and a whole history. The claim is just that you can imagine committing acts of terrorism.

This doesn't make it right. Of course. It doesn't make an act less evil if we can imagine how we could find our way around our inhibitions against it. It means that we can imagine situations in which we face an awful dilemma: commit terrorism or abandon something of deep value. The dilemma has an ironic similarity to dilemmas opponents of terrorism may face. Suppose that you are an officer trying to track down a terrorist planning an unspeakable act, such as an attack on a nuclear power station. You have apprehended the terrorist's family, who know where he is but will not tell you. You have to make them talk. How far will you go? Electric shocks, almost-drowning, pulling out toenails? To his wife? His mother? His children? These are awful acts. But the price for not performing them is high.

Terrorism often presents a special kind of moral dilemma, in which the choice is between an act that is evil and one that is wrong but not evil. In the fantasy of America occupied by sinister forces, the option of joining a campaign of assassination and bombing is evil, and the option of living quietly and letting your country decline in corruption and injustice is wrong but not evil. But this does not mean that a decent person should not choose the evil option simply because the alternative is merely wrong. A decent person should think long and hard before taking any such option, and should feel terrible about it afterwards. Sometimes a decent person will be unable to live with herself after doing what she had to do. Sometimes – not often, not in ordinary circumstances, and not without the very deepest reflection – you can be justified in crossing into the land of atrocity rather than putting up with something intolerable.

It could be right to choose the atrocious rather than the intolerable only if there were no other options. In imaginary cases we can rule out other options, but in real life it is usually a failing of moral imagination to think your options are so limited. The option that is overlooked usually involves non-violent moral leadership. Mahatma Gandhi and Nelson Mandela were faced with oppressive powers that had no intention of granting them rights. They waged long and patient campaigns: sit-ins, demonstrations, obstructions, vigils, disobedience. The theme of all these actions is their illegal lawfulness: violating the laws of the powerful but con-forming to moral principles with a scrupulousness that even the furious powers have to acknowledge. Call this general strategy the Gandhian option. This option, like terrorism, tests the patience of the powerful and invites violent reprisal. But, unlike terrorism, when the powerful take the bait and choose violence, it is against an innocent victim. The wrong-ness of the powerful has been transformed into evil. When a state's authority can only be maintained by inflicting atrocities on its citizens, it fades into something less than authority, mere power. So the Gandhian option presents the ruling state with a dilemma. Either it reacts brutally or it allows its laws to be disobeyed. It can survive neither without becom-ing something else.

That makes the non-violent option sound easy. But it is really very difficult and delicate, and often just not available. It requires that the state you are opposing be a real democracy or in some other way get its authority from its moral status. It requires that the powerless rebels have a cohesive social organization and be led by figures of moral authority. The leadership issue is crucial, I think. It takes a lot of persuasiveness to make impatient angry people hold back and act in concerted disciplined, non-violent, ways. When this has been possible, it has been due to leaders with an unusual combination of charisma and moral authority: Gandhi, King, Mandela. This is not something that can be produced at will.

In any case, the Gandhian option will often fail. One reason for failure is also a great strength. The Gandhian techniques are unlikely to succeed unless they are used for a cause that really does have right on its side. For they require that opponents, who have every reason not to get the point, see that their policies are wrong, or at any rate, begin to feel moral doubts that erode their capacity to act wholeheartedly. Recent philosophers have argued that sometimes an important part of the reason why an institution, such as slavery or patriarchy, changes is simply that it was wrong. When the arguments that would defend an institution cannot be found, even people who don't pay much attention to arguments find that their willingness to do what is needed to keep it in business is weakened. Or so it can be under some conditions, which it would be good to understand better. To take the Gandhian option you have to gamble that these conditions are satisfied, and that the rightness of your cause can see you through. You also have to gamble that your cause *is* right, or near enough to right that the inevitable compromises will work on a wider audience than those who already have faith in the cause. It is a strategy for neither the faint-hearted nor the dogmatic.

A metaphor: to take the Gandhian strategy you have to put your fate in the hands of God or Reason. If your cause is in fact just, these powers will see you through. But God or Reason sees further than you, and you can't second-guess their verdict.

In practical terms all these dangers are nothing compared to the likelihood that the powerful will win just because they are powerful. And then the campaign may bring much greater atrocity or injustice than the weaker people already face.

Acts of terrorism are usually committed by people with very limited power, strong convictions, and, they think, few options. Their acts can be justified only if their convictions are correct, their cause is overwhelmingly right, and if they really do not have other options. It is tragically hard to know when this is so. Anyone who says with confidence that, for example, if Palestianians want a state independent of Israel they have no options but terrorism is either bluffing or has some extraordinary information. The same goes for anyone who says with confidence that Palestinians have many promising non-terrorist options. The facts are heartbreaking and they are these: we can say with confidence that most acts of terrorism are terribly wrong, and we can say with less confidence that this "most" is not "all." We can also know that the cases where terrorism is justified are very very hard to distinguish from the cases where they are not. There may be one case in a thousand, and except at a level of knowledge that is rarely available except in hindsight, it looks like all the others.

FICTION VERSUS REALITY

So far I have been doing my best to tell the truth. I have described contexts in which real people do really evil things.

But evil deeds are done in books and films too, by fictional characters with fictional motives. We see life through stories. Our social lives and our politics are shaped by books, films, and legends; we learn history as a long thread of many stories. Stories can guide us or blind us.

Plots need villains, and the psychology of the villain has to fit the plot. No one knows what makes us respond to some narratives as particularly satisfying. The psychology of fiction must be closely connected to the psychology of psychologizing. That is, we must find roughly the same kinds of stories plausible when told as fictions and as accounts of what real people have done, and there must be close links between the plots we find particularly satisfying and the explanations we feel give our imaginations a good hold on real actions. But that doesn't mean that a good story really does give us insight into why people do things. Far from it. An appealing storyline can seduce us into thinking that people frequently act in ways they rarely do, and for reasons that seldom apply. The images current in our culture make us think that the murderer or rapist will be lurking in a dark alley or hiding in the bushes, when in fact he is more likely to be our spouse, our uncle, our sister-in-law. A parent's nightmares of pedophiles feature the archetype of Peter Lorre's character in M (the 1931 Fritz Lang film. The 1951 Joseph Losey remake is equally creepy) rather than the nice man next door. The fictional image is comforting, terrifying as it is, as it does not undermine our confidence in those near to us. And it evades the need to work our intuitive capacities hard, to grasp how a familiar personality can be capable of a heartless act.

Depictions of Nazi Germany and the Holocaust are a good example. They feature brutal camp guards, sadistic SS officers, and insane leaders. (The depiction of the camp commandant

Goeth by Ralph Fiennes in the 1993 Spielberg film of *Schindler's List* is a good example.) And of course all these existed, and were essential to what happened. But this depiction leaves out the essential middle element, the banal administrative component, of people marked by petty attention to detail, lack of imagination, and deference to authority. It would not be easy to make moving drama with a large cast of these more ordinary characters; and the more successful it was, the more disturbing it would be to many viewers. Not exciting-disturbing but confusing-disturbing: the horrible Nazis would seem too much like us.

I shall not discuss either of these examples. The only nightmares I will address are those of serial killers. I will focus on the Hannibal Lecter stories.

For a long time now we have had stories of detectives, who investigate murders. From Conan Doyle to Raymond Chandler to Ruth Rendell, the formula has been fairly standard. Someone has been killed and the reader has to ponder who is the killer. Much of the evidence concerns the motives suspects could have had, so that two kinds of interlocking puzzle are set. *Why* might this character have committed the crime, and *how* could she have managed to do it? Sherlock Holmes sets you to think mostly about How, and Ruth Rendell mostly about Why, but in all good detective stories "how" and "why" are closely wrapped around each other. As the genre evolved, the number of corpses per story tended to increase. Motive, though, when finally uncovered, tends to be relatively intelligible: someone wants something, someone doesn't want something uncovered, someone wants revenge. Sex and money, secrets and shame.

In the 1970s a new kind of murder came to public awareness, serial killings. There have always been serial killers, and

Jack the Ripper in Victorian London was a celebrated case, but the image of the serial killer did not come into popular consciousness as a distinct kind of nightmare until comparatively recently. The motives of a serial killer are harder to discern than in the kinds of murder that detective stories had usually described. And because of the mysteriousness of the motives, the topic is more fearsome. And the difficulty in understanding the criminal turns him into a diabolical monster, something like a vampire or a werewolf. The fictional image of a serial killer combines this half-human category with that of a more traditional killer, with motives and means that the detective has to uncover. The result is plots which combine an intellectual puzzle with a primeval horrified fascination.

There is a problem making fiction grow in this ground. Characters have to make some kind of sense, and the danger is that the criminal will turn out to be a force of nature rather than a motivated character. Villains without clear motives are not uncommon in literature. But psyching out the criminal is at the heart of detective fiction. The problem is solved brilliantly by Thomas Harris in the Hannibal Lecter novels. In each of them there are three main characters: a psychopathic serial killer, a detective, and Lecter. Lecter is himself a serial killer, but he is also a psychiatrist. He is in jail, and the detectives visit him to get his unique combination of first-person knowledge of serial killing and academic knowledge of psychopathology. There are two advantages of this device. Lecter can pronounce on the motives of the killer and though what he says may not make a lot of intuitive sense, we have his authority as a psychiatrist for it. And since he is not the central killer of the plot, he can be presented as a partly intelligible character: incredibly knowledgeable and awesomely sharp about other people's character and motives. We are also given a fairly trite psychological story about the central killer's psychology, involving unhappy childhood, gender confusion, and the like. This story would be disappointing and irritating were it not wrapped up in the authority and fascination of Lecter's personality. The killer's psychology is filtered through other people's theories of it; we don't have to deal with it directly. (There's a neat twist to this in *The Silence of the Lambs*. The killer believes falsely that he is a transsexual. Or so Lecter assures us. So we see the killer's mind through two lenses: we have Lecter's reliable account of the killer's own unreliable account of it.) In this psychological hall of mirrors it doesn't matter if the motives don't make sense.

There's a tug between intuition and rational thought here. Detective fiction has always involved the cold hard calculation of possible ways of committing and covering up a crime, and the warmer fuzzier sensitivity to criminal thoughts and emotions. (A good detective can have decidedly non-rational ways of getting at the rational processes of the criminal.) Philosophers of mind know very well how confusing the relation between thought and intuition can be. From the 1980s they have debated whether we understand other people by interpreting actions in terms of a theory, like a physicist explaining the motions of the planets, or whether we do it by reproducing their thoughts and feelings in our own minds. Developmental psychologists have got involved in the debate, and now we know a lot more about the ways small children can understand the minds of others. Most participants are now convinced that both explicit conceptual thinking and pure empathy occur and are essential, and that also much of our thinking about other people happens somewhere in a confusing and little-understood territory between these two.

The first of the Hannibal Lecter novels *Red Dragon* has a wonderful match with the theory/intuition debate in philosophy and psychology, which was just beginning when the book was written. The detective, an ex-FBI agent called Will Graham, has a gift of extraordinary intuition. He can absorb a crime scene and incidental facts about a killer until suddenly, in a way that he cannot understand, the killer's mind becomes live in his and he knows with intuitive certainty what kind of a person the killer is and what he will do next. It was he who captured Hannibal Lecter, by a leap of intuition. Lecter, brilliant as he is, years later is still deeply puzzled as to how Graham managed to catch him. He cannot understand how such a different person operates.

Lecter has a supernatural understanding of human motive and emotion, based largely on his almost superhuman intelligence, and no sympathy for human feeling. His remarks and letters to others show that he can hit the emotional bull's-eye in an uncanny way, and also that he has little capacity to put himself in another person's shoes. He is the ultimate sociopath, with no sense of what it is to be another person, but such a well-developed theory of human nature that he can fake it almost perfectly, and often accomplish what ordinary humans with their clumsy intuition and limited theories cannot. Unfortunately he also has a taste for human flesh, so the project of living successfully in the society of ordinary humans is not a simple one for him.

Hannibal Lecter thinks that he and Will Graham are kindred spirits, for he sees that Graham is a very intelligent person who can think like a sociopath. He thinks this means that at some level Graham must *be* a sociopath. He thinks this because he doesn't understand the difference between thinking about someone's mind and understanding it by simulating it in your own. He thinks that Graham predicts a killer's actions by thinking "what would I do?," ignoring the projection of one-self into another's situation which he himself is incapable of.

But the whole premise of the fiction is as implausible as Lecter's conjecture about Graham. In fact it is like that conjecture turned upside down. The books are based on the assumption that someone might get into the mind of a serial killer and understand intuitively its individual characteristics. So just as Lecter thinks that theory can do what we need intuition for, the Lecter novels suppose that intuition can do what we need theory for. And not just any old intuitive theory, but highly technical psychopathology. To do this, the novels need to postulate killers with individual themes and traits. Each killer targets a very particular kind of victim and kills in a way that works out a symbol of his particular style as a killer. Very few real killers are like this. Overwhelmingly, serial killers target a fairly wide class of victims, defined by gender, sexuality, and age, and then kill in whatever way comes easily to them. The signature usually consists in a way of finding the victim that the killer has learned will work for him, and sometimes a specific taste in sexual violence. When a real killer does have a distinctive signature, some unusual way of mutilating or disposing of bodies, the press seizes on the case, in large part because these comparatively rare cases are like the sensational characters in fiction.

The appeal of the idea that serial killers have very individual psychology as killers, a kind of artistic style that a sufficiently intuitive person could understand and anticipate, comes from thinking of them as both diabolically alien and also as rich characters. In the fictional genre of serial killers both assumptions are needed, but in fact serial killers are much harder to understand than this supposes. To begin with, sociopaths do not have exaggerated knowledge of human nature. They tend to develop a smooth social manner and to learn a number of conversational and social tricks, which work well with people who project imaginary personalities on the basis of a few behavioral hints. Dealing with a smooth sociopath is like interacting with the Eliza computer program, which by means of a few simple conversational moves fools you into thinking that you are interacting with a real sympathetic person. And although not all serial killers are full sociopaths, since some have a fair capacity for sympathetic understanding of other people, the same illusion applies. They function to some extent in the normal social world, and then they duck out of it for another part of their lives, in which they can function with a fixed repertoire of opportunistic tricks. Often they are loners, and when they have relationships these are often with other damaged people, who do not demand much mutual comprehension.

I am arguing that our image of the serial killer is shaped by fiction. The shaping is dangerous, in the following way. In the past a serial killer would find himself committing murders, be puzzled and often guilt-stricken, and would continue, as much a mystery to himself as to others. But now he may think "I'm a serial killer; I have a deep and interesting psychology; I have signatures and an individual style." So now he needs a signature and a style; he needs to commit his crimes in a characteristic manner that might attract a label and a myth. This might be beneficial, if it tempts a killer into predictable patterns and dangerous bravado. But there are also dangers. Grotesque signatures may make the killings even more awful than they would otherwise have been. The greatest danger is that the myth will produce killers. Someone who is not by nature a serial killer, but has violent fantasies mixed with confusion about his own place in the world, might seize on the glamorous persona of the fictional serial killer and set about becoming one. Such a person will be more likely to be caught than an opportunistic killer who acts when the occasion is right, but before he is caught, awful things will have happened.

MATCHING IMAGES

The Hannibal Lecter stories are right in one way. We think of our actions and those of other people through images. We see ourselves as lovers, strugglers, victims, and others as our lovers, our enemies, our oppressors. Fictional depiction of evil is potentially more revealing when it tries to capture the evil-doer's image of himself. The great danger of fictional evil is that it compresses into a few simple types the many very different ways in which we can overcome the barriers against harm. In reality, not only are there many ways to overcome the barriers, there are many images we use in overcoming them, and many ways we think of the others we harm. And the most serious harm comes from combinations of personalities, complementing one another in ways that are very hard to imagine. Think of terrorists again. A terrorist is likely to think of himself as a fighter for freedom and justice or a resister oppression. He will think of the people he opposes, his enemies and victims, as evil, as indifferent to the plight of his people. The pair of images may be like that described in the previous chapter: the terrorist thinks of the rulers as sociopaths and the rulers think of the terrorists as violent personalities or serial killers. There is a jigsaw pattern here, with four kinds of pieces: evil-doers' images of themselves and of their victims, their opponents' or victims' images of themselves and of the evil-doers.

There are really two patterns here. One is mirror-labeling. Two ethnic groups with a deep history of mutual atrocities each think of themselves as killers of monsters in defense of their families and think of the other as monsters. The other is jigsaw-labeling. Members of a powerful society whose comfort is disturbed by terrorists think of themselves as servants of just authority defending their families. This allows the terrorists to think of them as heartless functionaries driven only by obedience and partiality, and thus to think of themselves as fighters for justice, even for humanity. The labels of the two sides, though different, fit each other. The fact that each side uses the labels it does is part of the reason why the other uses the labels that it does. One protrudes where the other recedes.

There is an element of jigsaw-labeling even with much simpler evil, of the aggressor-and-victim kind. A serial killer thinks of his victims as sluts, garbage, snobs – some label that allows him not to think of them as human beings like himself. They think of him as an implacable monster embracing horror for its own sake. And however he thinks of himself, it will be in some way that is fueled by knowing how his victims label him. In the simplest form it is their fear fuelling his feeling of power.

Atrocity is real. Evil actions are real, really evil. The nightmares are not just in our heads. But what is in our heads, our images of evil, interact with reality in complex ways. Sometimes they help it happen, sometimes they simply mislead us about its nature. Our images let us down in two main ways. There are too few of them: we see all evil-doing as the same. This often blinds us to the nature of our own actions, as when terrorists think of themselves as patriots or strugglers against oppression, or when the complacently powerful think of themselves as defenders of decency. And they ignore the variety of personalities that usually combine to produce atrocity. The oppressed think of all the powerful as heartless and sociopathic, forgetting that they are dealing with a complex society which, like all societies, has its uses for soulless administrators and sadistic thugs. The powerful think that terrorists are all mindlessly violent, people who would be serial killers if they didn't have the excuse of a cause. They forget that terrorism too needs a mixture of ideologues, organizers, and activists, and that each of these has a different strategy for keeping the humanity of the other side out of consciousness.

All of these cases, and many more, appeal to a kind of imaginative laziness in us. We prefer to understand evil in terms of archetypal horrors, fictional villains, and deep viciousness, rather than to strain our capacities for intuitive understanding towards a grasp of the difficult truth that people much like us perform acts that we find unimaginably awful. A moving evocation of the difficulty of getting beyond crude images of evil is found in François Bizot's *The Gate* (2003), a description of his captivity by the genocidal Khmer Rouge. The book centers on the personality of a camp-leader and torturer, Douch. Bizot comes to understand, even to like Douch, while never losing sight of the fact that his actions are awful. Douch describes his activities to Bizot, who writes:

> Later, I often thought about this conversation: a dark revelation beneath a star of foreboding. . . . a huge part of my naïveté crumbled. Up till then, I had been convinced by the reassuring image of a brutal executioner. Now the man of faith, staring ahead of himself with an expression combining gloom and bitterness, suddenly emerged in his immense solitude.

Douch *is* a brutal executioner. So seeing him also as an individual person is disturbing. It means letting go of a reassuring, though frightening, image. The simple images are reassuring because they give us a simple false understanding instead of the deeper one that we can only with great difficulty attain.

Facing Evil: Reconciliation
Four

When an atrocity has been committed there are two things to do, one centered on thinking and one on emotion. We can try to understand why it happened, and we must find the right attitude to it, one that acknowledges its horror while allowing us to live our lives. There are many forms of understanding, and in earlier chapters I have been arguing that our capacities to understand evil are greater than we might think. There are also many different ways of acknowledging the magnitude of an evil. In her compelling book *The Atrocity Paradigm* (2002), Claudia Card argues that very often the emotional territory of forgiveness, amnesty, and reconciliation is as necessary as that of blame, punishment, and resentment. We do not realize this, says Card, because we do not appreciate the moral power of victims. In this last chapter I shall pull these two claims together, with the suggestion that the emotions we need in order to move on from an acknowledgment of evil require us to accept explanations of why the actions were committed.

The natural and traditional emotions towards people who have performed evil actions are anger, hatred, and desire for retribution. For good reasons. Very often they are the emotions that we can easily summon that allow us to deal with the situation. They come quickly and naturally, and they are often the only reactions available to people. So if victims are to have any appropriate reaction, anger and revenge are often the ones to have. Card does not deny this. Her suggestions are subtler and more interesting. She describes ways in which we can make a richer range of emotions available to us. We can do this by setting up situations, or designing institutions, which give us more opportunity to do justice to what has happened. An example of such an institution, though not one she discusses, is the Truth and Reconciliation Commission in South Africa. Card is arguing for a revised way of reacting to past atrocities. Similarly, I shall be arguing for a revised way of explaining evil actions. And just as it is part of Card's view that sometimes the appropriate reaction is rage, towards an action that is beyond forgiveness, so it is part of my view that sometimes the appropriate conclusion is that an action is beyond explanation.

INTUITIVE UNDERSTANDING

An explanation is something that makes us understand why something happened. There are many kinds of understanding. The simplest involve seeing a cause for an event: the house caught fire because the wiring was faulty. A more sophisticated explanation may appeal to the lack of causes: the die fell six-up three times in a row because random processes can sometimes result in unlikely strings of events. I am interested here in explanations that give intuitive understanding. Intuitive understanding is understanding that hooks up with our innate skills for dealing with practical problems. For example, an intuitive understanding of a physical phenomenon is one that fits into our natural sense of pushing and pulling things around: the tides happen because the moon's gravitational field pulls the oceans. My focus is on intuitive understanding of actions, where we explain what someone has done by linking it to the ways we have interacted with one another for millennia. For example, we explain why someone didn't apply for a job she had a good chance of getting by saying that she was afraid of rejection. Explanations like this come very naturally to us. They allow us to imagine what it is like to be the other person performing the action, and they give us suggestions about how we might influence the person, or how some shared activities with her might proceed. Of course, many explanations are not so intuitive. The explanation in physics of why there are two tides every day, one higher than the other, is much less intuitive than the explanation of why tides happen. And a psychological explanation of a criminal's action that says "people fitting this profile often perform acts of the following types" does not give you much sense of what it is like to be such a person, or what it would make sense to say or do on meeting one. Often that is the best we can get, if we want our explanations to be true rather than just comforting illusions. But this chapter is optimistic and adventurous: I am interested in our capacities for finding explanations that hook onto our intuitive social skills *and* have a chance of being true.

Intuitive understanding and moral disapproval tend to squeeze each other out. When we think that an act is wrong, we find it hard to imagine why the person did it. This is true even of our own actions. When you look back at something you are ashamed of, you often think, "How on earth could I have done that?" Usually you know the motive; you know that you acted out of lust, ambition, or envy. But why *that* motive made you overrule decency or prudence is in retrospect a mystery to you. The same goes for other people's sins: you usually know the motive but much less often why the motive was acted on. So when a kidnapper cuts off a child's ear and sends it to the worried parent, we know that this is done to show that the kidnapper does indeed have the child, and would not hesitate to harm her. But we don't know how the kidnapper manages to go on with it when the child begins to scream; we don't know what thoughts he finds to persuade himself that the child's terror doesn't matter.

When we don't know why a motive worked on someone, we do not know *how* he came to choose his action, though we know *what* he did and even a little bit of *why*. We cannot share his thinking and motivation. And that means we cannot imagine why he acted as he did. We can't stand in the shoes of the kidnapper, Stanley knife in hand, and pretend-decide to cut off the child's ear. We can't do this even if we were the kidnapper, years ago, and now the act seems to us horrible and inexplicable. This business of standing in imagination in someone else's shoes is very varied. It doesn't always require that we feel all the other person's emotions and sensations. That would be close to being the other person rather than simply understanding them. What it does require is that we run through some chain of thinking that corresponds to part of what is going on in the other person's mind. We have to be able to copy or mirror what they do when they work out what to think or what to do.

The simplest kind of imagination is something we learn when we learn to share actions with others. Games are a good example. Think of a game in which one child is trying to run past another without being touched. Each one feints and swerves and the other swerves and runs in response. To play this game you have to be constantly simulating the other person's preparations to move, to catch you or to avoid your catching them. As you do this, you get a vivid sensation of what it is like to be the other person. Adults get the same sensation from playing tennis, or chess, or making music. For that matter a good conversation is an adult equivalent of a chase game; you are always anticipating the other person's move, feinting, committing yourself once you see which way they're going. You're thinking for two, and so is the other person, and if it works you know that what is happening to you is happening to the other. This feeling of closeness is one of the main reasons we love doing these things.

Friendly interaction is not the only occasion for putting yourself in someone else's shoes, though. Sometimes we run through other people's thinking in order to trap or deceive them. The kind of imagining we do then is subtly different. It usually doesn't make you feel as close to the other person. This point is important because it suggests that we may think we can't have an intuitive understanding of someone because we are trying for the wrong kind of imagination. When you try to trap or deceive someone, you do get your mind to run along some of the same grooves as the other person's, but in a special way. If we want understanding to be compatible with condemnation, we shall need to consider kinds of understanding that preserve the distance between people. And, if what I am saying in this chapter is right, these kinds of understanding are available.

The central idea is simple. In much ordinary understanding we imagine ourselves into the desires of the other person. We imagine how we would act if we wanted what they want. But when imagining an evil action this should not be the aim because, as I have been arguing throughout, difference of desires is not the typical factor in evil. To imagine an evil action you have to imagine the person's way of turning their desires, which may be much like yours, into very different actions. We can begin to learn to do this.

Consider some easy cases of understanding an immoral action. I shall use Ronald Milo's classification of immoral actions, from his admirable book Immorality (1984). Milo classifies immoral actions under six headings. The full list is moral perversity, moral negligence, amorality, preferential wickedness, moral indifference, and moral weakness, but I shall only discuss moral perversity, preferential wickedness, and moral indifference.

Moral perversity is when a person accepts wrong moral principles. An example of great moral perversity would be convinced ideological racism. You may think that is hard to imagine, but consider something much less serious. You can easily imagine having a mild prejudice against people from some area. Perhaps you think of people from New York as pushy and overconfident, dishonestly presenting their own qualifications. You tend not to give jobs to New Yorkers. Then one year a New Yorker is transferred to your office who is gentle, tolerant, and as honest as the day is long. Looking back, you are puzzled about your own motives. Was the principle "stick up for honesty" or "down with New Yorkers"?

To use examples like these we need to see the continuity between the less serious cases and the awful ones; we need to see what this shows us about imagination. And we need to connect them with the concept of evil. We'll get to that; just wait a few paragraphs. Another of Milo's categories that applies to many cases of evil is preferential wickedness. That arises when a generally moral person doesn't give moral considerations enough weight in his thinking. An extreme case would be a general who adopts a strategy that results in thousands of enemy soldiers dying, where there is an alternative that would have given them a chance to surrender. His strategy may give a cleaner military victory, but at the price of many unnecessary deaths. Again the motive is clear, but try to imagine saying to yourself, "They're just soldiers, foreign soldiers, and if they don't die I'll only have vanquished, not routed, the enemy." You find that it sounds completely unconvincing: you can't add in the layers of ambition and carefully learned blindness needed to make that same thought clothe itself in other words. But, again, if you lower the moral stakes and move the topic nearer to your life, many real and easily imagined cases of preferential wickedness will come to mind. Any academic can imagine giving a bad book an even harsher review than necessary because it was written by someone from an opposed faction. ("Well, after all it is a bad book, and bad books pushing this line really ought to be discouraged.") Anyone in business can imagine filing for bankruptcy in a way that benefits shareholders rather than workers' pensions, when the workers belong to a union whose leadership has been partially responsible for the company's troubles.

Moral indifference, the last of Milo's categories that I shall consider, happens when a person knows perfectly well what she should do but completely ignores it when she acts. If we consider only single acts, there isn't a clear line between this and preferential wickedness. But if we shift attention to traits of character that result in whole patterns of action, there is a definite difference between someone who – hypocritically, self-deceivedly, or succumbing to temptation – gives insufficient weight to their duties to others, and someone who just never gives a damn about those duties. Someone who is this way throughout her life is a sociopath. We've seen numbers of sociopaths in the previous chapters. They are different from the normal run of humanity, though we will always have them among us. There is a gap here that is not going to be covered by ordinary imagination. But, still, there is a way. Remember from chapter three the idea that people in poor countries can easily see rich countries as sociopathic. And you can imagine a sociopathic country, indifferent to the plight of anything outside its borders, more easily than you can imagine a sociopathic individual. You can indeed imagine that something much simpler than a whole country – a company or a department or even a committee – can have this kind of indifference. So we have a metaphorical trick for grasping moral indifference: imagine being the chair of a committee, where one person always spouts moral platitudes while the rest of the committee always vote down anything this person proposes.

These examples have shown ways in which we can imagine being someone who has done something seriously wrong but not atrocious. They raise the hope of continuities our imaginations can follow, between everyday cases, cases of serious wrongdoing, and perhaps even worse cases.

IMAGINING EVIL

Now the hard part. We have to transform these hints about how to get intuitive understanding of moderately wrong actions into ways of intuitively understanding really evil acts. As I warned, the understanding is not going to be the same as the feeling you have for someone you are dancing with. It will be different because it will have to focus on something that we generally don't try to imagine, namely how a person overcame a barrier against considering atrocity. We generally do not imagine this, not because we never imagine doing actions that are in fact evil, but because the evil actions we routinely imagine are ones that people around us frequently perform, so that we just take for granted that the barrier can be overcome. A member of a slave-owning society might easily imagine how her friend was so annoyed at a slave for breaking something valuable that she had the slave beaten. Or for an example closer to home, consider the case of someone who has ample evidence that her husband is a serial rapist, but manages to explain it away, telling no one about the things that only she knows. Suppose that from time to time she briefly considers the possibility and then quickly, with a shudder, puts it out of her mind. We can imagine what is like to be this person, although what she does, cover up her husband's crime, is extremely wrong. We would do this by focusing on situations in which loyalty would make us hesitate to believe ill of someone central in our lives. But when we do this we don't notice how smoothly we have glided past the point at which she prevents herself from thinking "this is such a serious matter, I ought to think about it, and probably talk to someone."

We've seen in earlier chapters several resources for moving imagination along from ordinary wrongdoing to evil. One is imagining not the motivation itself but the image evil-doers have of their motivation. We can focus on the ideologies that can glorify brutality; the stories killers tell themselves about why they act. Another is imagining the fragility of a dangerous person's self-respect. We can focus on the unstable pride of a violent individual; the escape from depression that power over others can give. A third is imagining ways in which your own actions could be seen as evil. We can focus on how, as a well-meaning member of a rich society, you could be compared to a sociopath. (Remember, this focus is on how people could see you, not on how they could truly see you.) These are resources for imagining evil because they focus on specific ways in which we get around barriers to atrocity. See how each of them leads us step by step from the ordinary to the outrageous.

First, self-image. Everyone tells themselves stories about who they are, which allow them to manipulate their own motivation. Often this allows us to do things we couldn't otherwise do. To a child facing something scary you say "what a brave kid you are," hoping that getting the child to think of herself as brave will make her act bravely. We can manipulate ourselves this way to do wrong. There are many everyday examples. You have made a mess of a job at work, and you decide to pin the blame on a subordinate. You can only do this convincingly if you sack him. This won't be easy for you, since your relations have been friendly, and so you tell yourself, "I'm an ambitious person, and going places; one characteristic that marks me out for success is ruthlessness." Or consider a drug smuggler, imagining his actions in terms of the heroic images of the *narcocorrido* ballads that are now part of Latin American culture. He thinks he is like Robin Hood, or Indiana Jones, not the sleazy characters you read about in newspapers or see in films.

Now consider a horrendous example. Hannah Arendt in *Eichmann in Jerusalem* tells how SS officers, in order to make themselves capable of committing the horrors required of them, would think about how horrible their duties were:

> [T]he problem was how to overcome not so much their
> conscience as the animal pity by which all normal men are
> affected in the presence of physical suffering. The trick used
> by Himmler . . . consisted in turning these instincts around,
> as it were, in directing them toward the self: So that instead of
> saying: What horrible things I did to people!, the murderers
> would be able to say: What horrible things I had to watch in

> the pursuance of my duties, how heavily the task weighed
> upon my shoulders!

A thought like this is not inevitably linked to evil, for sometimes the right action is indeed repugnant. Remember the
example in chapter two of shooting an innocent-looking man
to save a child. Persuading yourself that you are the kind of
person who can do a repugnant act is playing with fire,
though. It can weaken barriers that ought to be left in place.

There are many cases between the ordinary wrong and the
horrendous here. It isn't necessary to string them out, because
the path from the one to the other is clear. If you can imagine
performing the ordinary wrong act, then you can imagine
using the same self-image manipulation to allow yourself to
perform the horrendous one. I'm not claiming that you can
imagine the full motivation of the horrendous act. But you
can imagine a crucial part of what makes it evil, the overcoming of an inhibition against harm.

Fragile self-respect is similar. We can imagine its barrier-
evading role for quite ordinary wrongdoing, and then think
in very similar ways about more drastic wrongs. There is a
universal human need to maintain self-respect, to think of
ourselves as valuable and in some way actually valued posi-
tively by others. But there is also tremendous variation in
what kinds of valuing will do the job. Some people need to be
loved, others to be feared, others to be thought of as morally
admirable. Whatever the value, we usually have contradictory
beliefs about it, with fantasies that sometimes function as
beliefs about how absolutely wonderful we are, and fears that
also sometimes function as beliefs about our utter worthless-
ness. That is the normal case, however sane one is. In some
people, though, the tension between being a god and being a

lump of dung is particularly unstable. Such people can need to go to extremes to maintain their sense of their own value.

But begin with a very ordinary case with very normal people. Everyday minor sadism. You are a kid in school and a particularly unpleasant and stuck-up teacher is about to sit down. There's a thumb tack on the chair, point upwards, and you do not warn her. In fact you watch in delight when she sits down on it, makes a face, tries to pretend nothing is wrong for a few moments, and then rushes out of the room.

It would be a peculiar child who did not enjoy this, though it is taking pleasure in someone else's pain. Where's the pleasure? It is essential that the victim is a teacher, someone who children think of as exerting power over them, and it is essential that the teacher struggle to preserve her dignity. The episode shows that the teacher is a vulnerable person like everyone else, like the children, so that they do not have to feel demeaned in comparison with her. Surely that is why it is fun to see the proud and powerful get their come-uppance, from banana peels to criminal charges. We don't get the same satisfaction from seeing the downfall of poor sinners such as ourselves.

How does this work? Why is one person's self-respect bolstered by the humiliation of another? It is one of the less attractive features of the species, and one of the more mysterious. There's a modicum of sanity in it: instead of setting ourselves impossible standards, we are content if we are as good as those around us. So we are more satisfied with what we have once we have brought down those who are happier than us. This helps explain envy, but it falls short of explaining sadism. But we don't need that kind of an explanation of it. As part of commonsense psychology, what we need is to use everyday envy to imagine it. The imagining transfers easily from cases like the teacher and the tack to much more sinister examples. Here is one.

All your life you have been in the shadow of a clever and ambitious contemporary. He does better than you at school, is a better athlete and musician, and eventually becomes a promising playwright. You on the other hand are a semi-employed reporter for an unknown paper, and your friend stays in touch with you to pick up little details of suburban life, always engaging with you in a tone that you find more than a little condescending. His first major play is about to appear off Broadway, and you happen to find yourself in a conversation with an editor of the NY Times, who happens to be wondering which of two critics he should send to review it. One is generally impartial and reflective, while the other is notoriously prone to instant enthusiasms or hates, and writes raves or vitriolic polemics. You have a sense that this second critic might not like your acquaintance's work, and you suggest that the editor assign him to review the play. The critic hates the play, and writes a devastating review, noting real faults and underlining them with gleeful contempt. When you read the review you chuckle with amusement at the humiliation of someone you have always envied. Your amusement turns to guilt a few days later when you learn that the bad review coincided with an unhappy turn in the play-wright's personal life and a dangerous moment in the cycles of his moods. He has killed himself.

The result is awful, and you should feel awful about your role in it. But you did not intend it. It takes only a few little changes to make the action really evil. Suppose that after the bad review you meet with the playwright, who is not too upset about it. So you point out the full sharpness of the barbs. Next time you meet he is a little more depressed, almost dangerously depressed. A malicious glee comes over you, and you point out that the problems of the play are not unrelated to the problems of his life. And so on, over a series of meetings. As he gets lower and lower, he turns to you more and more as someone to talk to, and you find more subtle ways of making him doubt his abilities and his future. (I'd have to write out the conversations to show exactly how "you" do it: a play, though not a very good one.) And then, not to your surprise, one day you learn of his suicide.

Your actions amount to murder. Murder driven by jealousy, fueled by admiration. If we move from the teacher and pin example through the first playwright story to this second story, we find our imagination transfers smoothly. You know what it would be like to maneuver your friend into killing himself. You know *part* of what it would be like, that is. You never know all of anything.

The third imaginative strategy I shall discuss is very different. It works by grasping how someone else might think that your motives are evil, seeing which aspects of your motivation this other person is focusing on, and then applying those aspects to other people. You imagine evil motivation by imagining aspects of your own motivation, using someone else's moral judgments to guide you. That sounds complicated, but there are simple examples.

You are an overweight North American, and you find what used to be a normal-sized car rather cramped. You buy an SUV, and find it a lot more comfortable. You don't feel so fat, driving around in something that fits you with the same spaciousness as the cars you drove as a teenager. Then you run into an eco-activist, who says, perhaps choosing slightly more tactful words than these, "you evil pig: polluting the air and depleting everyone's resources to remain fat; if you rode a bike you'd lose weight and do less harm. You're part of what's wrong with the world." This takes you aback, to put it mildly. You know that your choices can be criticized, but you have never thought of yourself as evil. Well, you don't have to come to a quick conclusion on that to make some use of the comment. You can use it to give you an intuitive hold on other people.

Consider an act of callous negligence, based on a real case in 2003. A driver is returning home when a vagrant falls drunk off a bridge and strikes the windscreen of her car. Instead of stopping, she drives home with the man still embedded in the windscreen, goes indoors to satisfy her drug habit, and does not return for several hours, by which time he has bled to death. The act seems incredible, unimaginable. But compare it to your SUV purchase. You hear talk of the environment, like the groans of the man in the windscreen, and you realize, though you put it out of your mind, that your actions are part of a pattern that will have bad consequences. But in order to act otherwise you would have to live a different kind of life, free of refined sugar and processed fats. Perhaps you would like to do that eventually, but the withdrawal symptoms if you did it suddenly would be rough. So you put off any action to remedy the situation until some future time.

There are real psychological similarities between this person and "your" situation in the SUV-buying case, though there are equally real differences. You can use them to get some understanding of the incredible callousness of the person in the story. From her point of view, the man in the windscreen was a bad situation to be addressed somehow, just as you think the state of the environment is. But for neither of you is the badness of the situation as vivid as the needs of the moment. And for both of you the problem of figuring out what best to do about the bad situation means that you find ways of perpetually pushing it out of your consciousness.

The psychological similarity may not make a moral similarity. You are not directly involved in any particular person's death. You have not seen with your own eyes the damage that is being caused. You are not uniquely placed to help someone and refusing to. These differences may be crucial, morally. That is for you to decide. You may decide that you were right all along: your acts are open to fair criticism but are not evil. Even if that is what you decide, seeing how someone could bring an intelligible charge of evil against you that did not misconstrue your motives gives you a tool for understanding some evil actions of some other people that you would otherwise have found unintelligible.

RECONCILIATION: THE SOUTH AFRICAN CASE

The forms of understanding I have been discussing are all partial. They leave as much mysterious as clarified. In fact that is true of any intuitive explanation we ever give. But the explanations I have been describing leave unexplained some aspects that we are not used to leaving mysterious. And they go into more detail of other aspects that we do not usually need to say much about. What is the point of trying for these kinds of fractional understanding? My answer to this question involves a detour. This section is about reconciliation. You'll see the connections later.

When South Africa made its historic transition to democracy in 1994 its people could look back on decades of horror. In the previous decades of apartheid, the rule of a minority of whites, in the face of well-organized, patient, and utterly determined movements towards equal rights for all citizens, could only be maintained by systematic brutality. There is no need to repeat the full catalog. This was a government that practiced interrogation by blowtorch, the routine murder without trial of political opponents, the shooting of children, and in which police officers could have a cheerful barbecue beside the body of a political prisoner they were burning. The resistance was also violent. There were bombings, assassinations, and mob violence. Thus when the apparatus of repression finally collapsed, it was not at all obvious how people of such varied convictions and from ethnic groups between which such bitterness had grown could work together to make the country function. And there was a real danger that the settling of scores would produce an era of atrocity in which the main victims would be the formerly powerful. South Africa escaped these dangers in the years immediately following the transition. There was less violence than anyone had expected and a remarkably general cooperation in building a new society. One reason for this escape was the Truth and Reconciliation Commission, set up by an act of the new South African Parliament with legally enforceable powers but an aim that was much wider than that of any conventional legal proceeding. The core idea was that individuals could appear before the Commission and admit to violations of the rights of others during the years of oppression. The Commission could investigate their acts and call other witnesses. If it thought that the applicant had dealt with it truthfully and in an attitude conducive to reconciliation, it could grant an amnesty, freeing the applicant from fear of criminal charges over his or her actions.

The Commission had a remarkable success. Many people appeared before it, and their testimony threw enormous light on what had been going on in the preceding years. The families of many victims now knew what had happened to their relatives, and at whose hands they had died. This information might have been expected to produce rage, but the usual reaction was relief and an abatement of years-old anger and grief. Very often victims and torturers met and accepted one another as people who had been trying in different ways to get through hard times.

The only real failure of the Commission was its inability to get the top figures in the former government to testify. This was a significant gap, since the police and army officers who testified usually represented themselves as cogs in a machine which they now could see as evil, but which was directed from above. And indeed there was evidence that the leaders of the nation had a greater knowledge of the detail of atrocities than is usual in democratic states. The old South Africa was at best a marginal democracy, but there was a somewhat free press and a façade of democratic institutions. In democracies leaders usually prefer to keep several layers of ignorance and unaccountability between themselves and the details of crimes that they have set up but not literally committed. But it seems, for example, that the South African President authorized the bombing of the headquarters of the South African Council of Churches. So the lack of involvement in the Commission of the former leaders meant that a significant part of the past was left open to factual speculation and emotional ambiguity.

The South African Commission was certainly not the first occasion in which a society has looked back on its past with the aim of enabling former enemies to live together. A famous example is the amnesty in Athens in 403 BCE, in which after a revolution that restored democracy by overthrowing the rule of a group of thirty tyrants, the Athenians resolved not to pursue one another for their roles in the tyranny and the revolution. The victorious democrats swore an oath which included the clause "I will harbor no grievance against any citizens, save only the Thirty . . . and even of them against none who shall consent to render account of his office." Again we see the link between truth and reconciliation: if the ex-tyrant will say what he has done and why he did it, his actions will not be held against him. The Athenian amnesty seems to have built on a tradition of similar measures in ancient Greece, meant to break cycles of vendettas and retributions. And often in human history people must have thought that in order to prevent endless cycles of atrocity, they must renounce their rights to retribution. In modern times the idea has usually surfaced at times when a society not only looks back on a period of horror, but is dealing with considerable uncertainty about what has actually happened. An early example was the National Commission on the Disappeared, a commission set up by the government of Argentina in 1983 to investigate the massacres and kidnappings that occurred under the previous military dictatorship. There are now at least fifteen examples of commissions set up to investigate human rights abuses as a way of enabling a country to come to terms with its past.

The South African case is special, though. It combined an unusual number of features essential to real reconciliation. The central features were the following:

- It was not a court. Not only did it not have the power to punish, its concern was with violations of human rights in general, whether or not they were crimes or legally excusable.
- It was backed up by the power of the state. It could subpoena witnesses, and lying to it was perjury.

- It could award compensation to individuals after determining their losses. These compensations were usually small and symbolic in comparison with the losses. Money does not bring back your child. But they functioned as a gesture of apology to those who had been wronged. It could also recommend other gestures of recognition, such as the naming of streets after victims.
- It did not require that an applicant for amnesty express contrition or feelings of guilt, though applicants could not be proud of their actions or indifferent to the sufferings of their victims. It required them instead to accept that what had happened was awful, and that the victims were victims.
- It was concerned with all atrocities committed by all participants. Most of its members and most of South African society must have thought that the acts of those opposing the former regime were more justified than those of the regime – but for the Commission, an atrocity was an atrocity.
- Its primary aim was to discover the truth. The main duty of an applicant for amnesty, or anyone else who testified before it, was simply to give a full and accurate account of what had happened.

The South African experience has inspired other attempts at reconciliation. The usual context is a successful transition to democracy after a period of despotism or chaos. There have not been successful imitations in societies where no such transition has taken place, either because of the absence of democracy or because the society has always been basically democratic. There has been no such exercise in Northern Ireland, for example, though there too both sides of a divided society have inflicted many atrocities and there too many questions remain unanswered, fueling suspicion and uncertainty. There are enormous barriers to setting up any such commission where there has not been a fundamental change of regime, since government agencies will fight hard to preserve the secrecy of their activities. And often even when a society has gone through a fundamental upheaval, the kind of reconciliation we are discussing is blocked by the symbiotic motives to keep things in the dark and for revenge. In Europe after the Second World War, the past was dealt with by a superficial dose of victors' justice, as in the Nuremberg trials and the prosecutions of collaborators in France, followed by a collective amnesia. Only decades later were there systematic attempts to bring the facts and the personalities into the public arena, once post-war society had already taken shape.

Reconciliation does not require a government-sponsored commission. There are non-governmental organizations devoted to reconciliation in specific domains. An important one is MVFR, Murder Victims' Families for Reconciliation, an organization of relatives of murdered people, of which I am a member, which campaigns to make the point that not all people affected by violent crime would find vengeance comforting. The MVFR is an important element in the campaign against capital punishment in the USA, where it is often assumed that relatives of murder victims would be outraged if those convicted of their murders were not executed. As far as I know, no equivalent organization exists in the UK, where it is assumed that the relatives of murder victims, particularly the parents of murdered children, assert a power for vengeance that politicians have to negotiate very carefully.

RECONCILIATION VERSUS FORGIVENESS

Reconciliation is not forgiveness. It has a deeper aim. One forgives a person for an act she has committed, where it is taken for granted what she has done, and where it is agreed to act as if the act had never occurred. The ideal case of forgiveness follows true repentance, where the wrong-doer understands the wrongness of her actions and has changed in ways that make her unlikely to repeat her actions. So then one can resume social life with her, ignoring her past personality: "forgive and forget." Or more often, forgive and make a show of trying to forget. Many acts are beyond forgiveness: no one would have the presumption to forgive the Nazis for the Holocaust. Even if the state of Israel on behalf of the Jewish people were, incredibly, to make some such declaration, it would be a sham. No one would believe it and the very intention would be offensive. This is not something the human race must ever agree to forget, or even in some lesser way to act as if it had not occurred. As Arendt and others have argued, there is a worrying paradox here: some acts are beyond forgiving, but they are beyond punishment too, as nothing one could do to individual perpetrators would be proportional to what they had done.

Reconciliation is different. One is reconciled with a person, not with their actions, and one does not act as if the actions had not been performed. To be reconciled with a person is to accept that person as someone with whom one could cooperate in shared projects, placing aside feelings of hostility or injury that might make such cooperation impossible. In particular, one renounces the desire to punish or to get even. This does not mean that one ceases to think that the person has done wrong, or that one feels affectionately towards him. One simply takes him as another human being with whom one can to some extent look towards the future. This is easiest when the recovery from evil is central among the shared future-directed projects, when the reconciled people can work together to heal a society or make individual lives move forward.

A troubled couple can be reconciled with each other, as a means to continuing a family life. This is something they can decide to do, if they can make sense of each other's intentions to do it. Forgiveness can come later. Perhaps it will never come, in which case it might be better not to continue the relationship. But even if they separate, they may well need to deal with each other, for example to discuss their children. Then too reconciliation is what they need: an attitude of separating the aspects of each other's personalities that they can and cannot accept, with a strategy for a reduced social life with those that they can. (Talk of forgiveness sometimes makes me think of the last scene of Mozart's *The Marriage of Figaro*, when the Countess forgives the Count for his infidelities and the chorus sings "everyone is content," though the characters and the audience all know that no one has changed, and the situation will recur as soon as a chance arises.)

Nelson Mandela put the point very sharply. In a preface to a book of essays about the Truth and Reconciliation Commission entitled *Commissioning the Past* (2002), he wrote of

> identifying the nature and scope of past wrongs and taking methodical steps to remove them. I believe that joining hands in that task is a central aim of reconciliation. I am often asked how it is that I emerged without bitterness from so long a time in prison. . . . [M]illions of South Africa's people spent an even longer time in the prison of apartheid. Some were imprisoned by the apartheid laws in a condition of homelessness and near-despair. Others were imprisoned in the racism of the mind. These are places where some still languish. . . . In such circumstances, personal bitterness is irrelevant. . . . Instead

we must insist with quiet resolve on a firm policy of undoing
the continuing effects of the past.

Reconciliation is both more and less than forgiveness. More
in that it requires a change of attitude on both sides, with each
recognizing the motives of the whole other person, and less in
that it does not require that either person cease to condemn
the actions of the others. Both sides must now have enough
understanding of the other that they can cooperate in a shared
project of "undoing the continuing effects of the past." That is
why we can be reconciled to evil though we cannot forgive it.

There is a rich set of contrasts between reconciliation and
forgiveness. They form part of a family of attitudes to people
who have done wrong. The family can be arranged in a series:
rehabilitation, pardon, forgiveness, reconciliation. The simplest attitude is rehabilitation, where one accepts the person
into society ignoring what their crimes may have been and in
what ways they may be guilty. Stalin's victims were "rehabili-
tated" into later Soviet society, sometimes posthumously. The
most complex is reconciliation, which I am trying to clarify.
There are other families of attitudes with important parallels
to this one. The most significant can also be arranged in a
series: shame, regret, guilt, remorse. Here too shame is the
simplest. In its basic form it consists simply in awareness that
others will condemn one. And remorse is the most complex.
There are deep connections between the two families.

Emotionally sophisticated people do not simply blunder
into their feelings but make some effort to have the emotions
appropriate to their situation. An emotionally sophisticated
person will not call for forgiveness when reconciliation is
more appropriate (or vice versa). Nor will an emotionally
sophisticated person feel guilt when remorse is what is called

for. In fact this latter case has important connections with the relation between forgiveness and reconciliation.

People often feel guilt when it would be better to feel remorse. The best examples are those in which someone has made a difficult choice in a moral dilemma. Suppose a man steps out of the dark to stop your car. You drive on quickly, even though you see that he is being chased by other men. They are criminals, and kill him. Any responsible person would have tortured thoughts after such an incident. But they can take an irrational form "I am bad; I should suffer for this." The rational form is "I wish I had been capable of finding other ways out of situations like that." It is a form of intense regret, rather than remorse or guilt.

It takes emotional maturity to be able to find the right emotion at such moments, the one that does justice to the awfulness of the situation without unnecessary self-punishment. Individual people cannot find such accurate emotions all by themselves; they need the support of a culture in which the contrasts between the emotions are made vivid. We are capable of keeping guilt and regret apart. We are also capable of keeping forgiveness apart from reconciliation. Suppose that the family of the man in the road accuses you, the driver who didn't stop for him, of failing to save his life. They may think that even though it would have placed your own life at risk, you ought to have taken that risk to save someone who was obviously in mortal danger. You disagree, though privately you play and replay the situation to see whether there is something else you could have done. They may never forgive you. But they can be reconciled to you. To do this they have to understand how you were thinking in the crucial situation, and how you see it in retrospect. You and they may continue to disagree about what you should have done, but you can both accept each other's way of thinking as points on the spectrum of human possibilities, which can fit together in constructive social life.

The act in the example was not evil, though depending on the details it may have been a moral mistake. The situations of many evil-doers are paradoxically like those of people caught in moral dilemmas. That is, they *feel* to the participants as if they face ghastly choices where there will be deep grounds for remorse whatever they do. In fact, this is an illusion: there are courses of action open to them that they have no moral choice but to take. Consider a policeman in the old South Africa whose job requires him to torture prisoners. If he does not do this he will be out of a job, unable to support his family, and branded as a subversive, becoming at best unemployable and at worst made a prisoner himself. He overcomes his resistance, in order as he sees it to survive in difficult times, and starts down the long road to getting actual satisfaction out of destroying others. From the outside, with hindsight, we think this was wrong. Not just the obvious mistake about what he should have done, but a deeper mistake: he thought that there was no easy summing up of the pros and cons of the options open to him. But we now think, and looking back he may also now think, that in fact there was only one defensible action. He should have refused, whatever the consequences.

Reconciliation in this case cannot consist in the victims or relations saying, "We would have chosen differently, but that was your choice." Nor even in saying, "We think that was wrong but we accept that you were trying to do right." These are infinitely too mild, since the policeman had stumbled into serious wrong, real evil. What they can say is, "We understand the course of thinking that took you to this evil place; we see its seductive quality; what you did was unforgivable, but we understand how human beings can be led to such terrible things."

Reconciliation, as I am describing it, requires something from both sides. I have been describing cases in which there is a clear "perpetrator" side and a clear "victim" side. Often both sides are perpetrators. Or, even harder to resolve, each side thinks that they are the victims and the others are the perpetrators. There's usually little hope of getting agreement on who was the perpetrator in such cases. Or even of getting agreement that the question may not be worth resolving. But often each side should be able to see that the other was in a situation that felt like a moral dilemma. It felt as if they were faced with difficult choices with no clear moral way through. Then reconciliation is possible, each side can try to understand enough of the motivation of the other that they can both take part in "a firm policy of undoing the continuing effects of the past."

ONE-SIDED RECONCILIATION

I have discussed reconciliation in terms of the need of two individuals or groups to get on with a partially shared life. But even in the cases I have described, the situation is often not symmetrical. Often one person is the perpetrator and the other the victim. Then too there are very hard questions about what attitudes to take. What is it reasonable to feel towards someone who has done something awful to you or to someone you love? What emotion should you feel towards yourself when you realize the enormity of what you have done to someone else? My remarks on this are tentative and exploratory.

The answer that comes naturally to humans is that rage and hatred are the response to an atrocitor, self-directed hatred if the atrocitor is you. These attitudes are extensions of our attitude to smaller-scale offenses. If someone hits you or deliberately breaks something of value to you, it is not only easy to respond with anger, it is functional. You defend yourself, and you threaten the other person in a way that makes it less likely that the offense will be repeated. And up to a point it makes sense that the greater the injury, the greater the anger. But beyond a point it ceases to make sense. The obvious angry response to murder is to kill the murderer. But a person can only die once, so we are left with no scaled-up response to multiple or atrocious murder. One traditional response is to kill not only the murderer but also his family, or to kill him in some particularly gruesome way. But the price for this has become too high: we cannot do this while keeping our own self-respect. In extreme cases it just isn't possible to feel an appropriate amount of anger; it would kill us.

Moreover, anger is a response of the moment. It does not turn easily into an attitude that can guide one over a period of time. And, as a hot momentary feeling, when it becomes a long-term attitude, hatred, it becomes corrosive. In particular it tends to block off the past, and prevent people from remembering what exactly happened. In fact it has a dogmatic tendency: it tends towards reinforcing a fixed opinion rather than piecing together what actually happened, and why. When you hate, you know whom you hate and it is part of the hate that they must be responsible in the way you want them to be.

At this point we connect with the idea of truth. The victim wants to be able to bear witness, not simply to support a prosecution, but as part of an inquiry into the true facts of the matter. Primo Levi writes of the common nightmare of camp inmates of eventually escaping and then "telling their story and not being listened to." Perhaps the Christian idea of a final judgment is attractive in part for this reason. Eventually everyone's story will be told. One reason, I am sure, why we search for the truth about the unreconciled past is to find ways out of anger that is more than we could bear. It is revealed in such things as the sense of enormous relief in the Soviet Union when Solzhenitsyn's *One Day in the Life of Ivan Denisovitch* was published in *Novy Mir* in 1962. Finally someone had said it. One thing we are searching for in the truth about the past comes under the general label of reconciliation. We want to get some intuitive understanding of how another person – sometimes oneself – could have done what they did.

The practical and the emotional are closely entwined here. Sometimes we have to deal with someone we cannot forgive, and then we have to isolate those parts of their motivation that we hold responsible, and which will not change, while seeing within the rest of the person something to deal with. An abused wife, for example, may need to fix in her mind her ex-husband's rages, while separating them from his love for his children, with which she can negotiate. And even when there is no need for actual contact, the person is still there in our heads, and we need to do something similar in order to exorcize this threatening and haunting presence. If we do not, we are either eaten up by our own rage or robbed of the past by our efforts to contain it.

It never succeeds, not fully. No sane person ever comes fully to terms with something awful they have done, nor something awful that someone else has done. And no single person can invent the resources to do it. A whole culture has to explore the emotional resources that it may make available to its members. I would want the philosophy of mind to be part of that exploration.

EVIL-RESISTANT INSTITUTIONS?

When atrocities have occurred, we need to recover from them, to get on with our lives. And we ought to do what we can to ensure that we are not implicated in future atrocities. A theme of this book has been the potentiality of normally benign institutions such as democracy and religion to facilitate evil: you should not be too confident that because your values are firm and you are a member of a fundamentally good society, you could not find yourself playing some part in a major evil. Members of German society early in the twentieth century had every reason to think that they were among the most civilized and decent people on earth. Even a very small probability of something sufficiently awful is worth taking very seriously. So, looking back with horror and looking forward with apprehension, we might ask ourselves how a society can equip itself to deal with the human capacity for evil.

Institutions for coming to terms with past evil and for protecting against future evil are generally very similar, I think. Consider a radical idea. At present we deal with crimes through criminal and civil law. The criminal law is directed at punishment. Its role is to deter future offenses, to segregate dangerous individuals, and to give victims a sense that their sufferings have been addressed. The civil law is directed at righting wrongs, particularly financial wrongs. Its role is to undo the effects of illegal actions, to order individuals and companies to change their ways, and to some extent to compensate for non-financial losses. The range of roles played by the civil law is even greater than that played by the criminal law. Consider a suit for damages brought against a hospital by the parents of a baby who died as a result of medical negligence. The tragedy has in fact saved the parents the expense of raising and educating the child, though only the most callous and clumsy of defense lawyers would mention this in opposing the suit. The parents' purpose in bringing the suit is to punish the hospital financially as a way of relieving their anguish, and to bring to light the facts of the matter, which the hospital is likely to have done its best to obscure. But a legal process whose primary function is to compensate for financial losses is not well designed to do either of these things. The proceedings are unlikely to bring the parents any sense of emotional closure, and the knowledge that revealing too much is likely to make the settlement more costly gives the hospital an incentive to react with reluctance to the parents' need for facts. Situations like these require a different kind of institution.

Suppose that whenever an atrocious crime is committed, victims could require a special court of inquiry. The right to call for this inquiry would be restricted to real atrocity, involving death, extreme suffering, rape, and the like. The function of the court would not be to impose punishments or to award damages but to bring the facts to light. Rape victims could establish the full extent of their aggressors' activities, and the extent to which their activities were tolerated by the authorities. The parents of the child killed by medical negligence could expose the working practices of the hospital, the way doctors covered up for their incompetent colleagues, and so on. The family of a murder victim could inquire into the motives as well as the acts of the murderer, could make public other crimes linked to the murder, and could strive for mutual comprehension with the murderer's family. Such courts could subpoena witnesses, and testimony would be subject to the penalties for perjury. But the aim would be completely different from either a criminal or a civil case as we now know them. Participants would have to accept that no punishment inflicted on a criminal nor any monetary compensation brings back a dead loved one, or makes their suffering any less acute. They would have to refocus their distress on discovering and understanding.

Such an institution would ask why atrocities happen. Its role would be to ask awkward questions, and to provide a space where emotions could be expressed and tamed. It would be an exercise in enlightening emotion, keeping separate the different attitudes one can have to the past, and in applying ways of imagining evil motivation like the ones discussed in this chapter. It would come into its own most of all in cases where people have harmed one another and each thinks the other is the one that has acted wrongly. Each considers themselves to have been in a dilemma in which some normal barrier to harm had to be overcome, and each considers the other to have bypassed some barrier that ought to have been respected. Each thinks, "I feel regret but not guilt – as for him, it is guilt he should feel." That's when you really need reconciliation. You need institutions, and a culture that sees the point of the institutions, in which people can compare their own innocent motives to other people's guilty ones, and can understand how others could see their motives as guilty.

At this point reflection on the past and protection against the future come together. We can begin to see what a society would be like in which the emotions available to people – in the family of remorse, in the family of blame, in the family of reconciliation – can combine with intuitive psychological continuities between acceptable and repugnant acts to give more resources for facing past evils and anticipating future ones. We would be better equipped to detect and resist the infiltrations of evil into our lives. Not perfectly equipped, as we never could be, but with a better capacity to understand this fundamental aspect of life.

Notes

ONE EVIL AND OTHERNESS

Introduction

For twentieth-century horrors see Martin Gilbert, Holocaust, NY, Holt, Rinehart & Winston, 1986; Ben Kiernan, Pol Pot Regime: race, power and genocide in Cambodia under the Khmer Rouge 1975–79, New Haven, CT, Yale University Press, 2003; Romeo Dallaire, Shake Hands with the Devil: the failure of humanity in Rwanda, Toronto, Random House Canada, 2003; and Jonathan Glover, Humanity: a moral history of the twentieth century, New Haven, CT, Yale University Press, 2001. To lessen the impression that the twentieth was a uniquely awful century, see Barbara Tuchman, Distant Mirror: the calamitous fourteenth century, New York, Knopf, 1978; and Robert Gellately and Ben Kiernan (eds), Spectre of Genocide: mass murder in historical perspective, New York, Cambridge University Press, 2003.

My use of the term "atrocity" is influenced by Claudia Card's The Atrocity Paradigm: a theory of evil, New York, Oxford University Press, 2002. Atrocity is not the same as evil. Atrocity is a property of events, and is measured in suffering, death, and humiliation. Evil is a property of actions, and then of people, and is determined by the way in which they tend to produce atrocity. Card shows us how hard it is to get clear about the relation between atrocity and evil.

My allusion to Kant is to his discussion of "the radical evil in human nature" in Religion within the Limits of Reason Alone, translated by Theodore H. Greene and Hoyt H. Hudson, New York, Harper & Row, 1960. The tag "radical evil" is misleading. Kant is not discussing any extreme depravity, but rather the depth to which the to him inexplicable tendency to do any wrong, however slight, is found in human nature.

How "evil" makes evil

For the fundamental attribution error see Richard E. Nisbett and Lee Ross, *The Person and the Situation*, New York, McGraw-Hill, 1991. Consequences of Nisbett and Ross's work for our concepts of personality have been drawn by Gilbert Harman, "Moral philosophy meets social psychology: virtue ethics and the fundamental attribution error," *Proceedings of the Aristotelian Society*, 99, 1999, pp. 315–31. See also John Doris, *Lack of Character: personality and moral behavior*, Cambridge, Cambridge University Press, 2002 and Peter Goldie, *On Personality*, London, Routledge, 2004.

The dangerousness of the concept of evil has been pointed out by a number of writers. See for example Roy C. Baumeister, *Evil: inside human violence and cruelty*, New York, Freeman, 1997, and Aaron Beck, *Prisoners of Hate*, New York, HarperCollins, 1999. An example of the need of people to see those they are mistreating as evil is given in Solzhenitsyn's description in part V of *The Gulag Archipelago* (New York, Harper & Row, 1978) of how camp guards came to see their prisoners as nefarious and dangerous.

Evil versus wrong

The distinction between the English words "evil" and "wrong" is a subtle one and depends a lot on the context in which the term is used. Nietzsche's contrast between *"schlect"* and *"böse"* is often translated as one between "bad" and "evil," though *"böse"* has a wider range of meanings than "evil." *"Übel"* is more like "evil" than *"böse"* is. In French the word *"mal"* used as an adjective tends towards wrong/bad, with *"maléfique"* being used for evil, and as a noun tending to mean "evil." In late Latin a distinction appears between *"malus,"* which covers all kinds of wrong, and *"maleficus,"* which applies to evil. It is interesting that *"maleficus"* has connotations of activity: disposed to make wrong. Though I hesitate to put it dogmatically, I have the firm impression that characters in Greek tragedy are not to be taken as evil. Evil characters, as opposed to simply violent or malevolent ones, appear first in European literature about the time of Seneca's tragedies. It has been argued that the concept of evil is absent in classical Chinese thought. See Roy W. Perrett, "Evil and human nature," *The Monist*, 85, 2002, pp. 304–19, and Bryan Van Norden, "Mencius and Augustine on Evil," in Bo Mou (ed.), *Two Roads to Wisdom? Chinese and analytical philosophical traditions*, Chicago, Open Court, 2001. It is plausible, then, that the concept of evil arises in the west around the time of Stoicism and Christianity. It then becomes a central concept in

European philosophy, as charted in Susan Neiman's *Evil in Modern Thought*, Princeton, Princeton University Press, 2002.

There is an evocative description of the incredulity of victims in the chapter "Evil beyond vice" of Raimond Gaita's *A Common Humanity*, London, Routledge, 1998. Using a quotation from Simone Weil, Gaita asks what it is about humans, as distinct from animals, that makes them surprised when horrors are inflicted on them.

Truman versus Milosevic

For the dropping of the first atomic bombs see Barton J. Bernstein (ed.), *The Atomic Bomb: the critical issues*, Boston, Little, Brown, 1976, and Dennis Wainstock, *The Decision to Drop the Atomic Bomb*, Westport, CT, Praeger, 1996. Recent work makes it clear that there was no shortage of bombs. A demonstration would not have left the US with no further bomb to use.

The point of this section should not get bogged down in details of how many died, what alternatives were really viable or what were the foreseeable longer-term results. These are not really relevant to what I am arguing, which is not as much a contrast between the actual men Truman and Milosovic as between moral miscalculation from decent motives and accurate calculation on awful motives. The point is that major disparities of this kind can easily happen. An easier case to make is that the Truman of my invention did something worse than a minor war criminal, such as the Bosnian Serb Arkan, or a less powerful evil politician, such as the Bosnian Serb leader Radovan Karadžic.

Evil and intelligibility

The quotation is from Bernhard Schlink, *The Reader*, translated by Carol Brown Janeway, New York, Vintage Books, 1995.

For data relating explaining and condoning see Arthur G. Miller, Anne K. Gordon, and Amy M. Buddie, "Accounting for evil and cruelty: Is to explain to condone?," *Personality and Social Psychology Review*, 3, 1999, pp. 254–68.

My account here might seem to be taking sides between philosophers who stress imaginative simulation in understanding others and those who stress learned and innate theories. No: that debate is about what is primitive; both sides agree that often when we understand we imagine, but one side thinks that we imagine by applying a theory.

The demonic image

The doctor case is meant as a counter-example to the account of evil in Colin McGinn's *Ethics, Evil, and Fiction*, Oxford, Oxford University Press, 1997. Though I disagree with McGinn on the crucial issue of how to characterize evil motives, his book does have the insight that our concept of evil is based largely on fictional cases. He does not consider, though, the consequence that this may give it a tendency to misdescribe real cases. One might be attracted to an alternative approach, of providing a clear and consistent description of someone to whom the demonic image might apply. Daniel Haybron has explored this in a number of papers. See "Moral monsters and saints," *The Monist*, 85, 2002, pp. 260–84, and "Consistency of character and the character of evil," in D. Haybron (ed.), *Earth's Abominations: philosophical studies of evil*, New York, Rodopi, 2002. Haybron is pushed to the conclusion that Hitler was not evil, because he had some non-evil human relationships, and that the fictional Tony Soprano is not a depiction of evil because he is a devoted family man.

Temptation

The divide between understanding actions in terms of the rational satisfaction of a person's whole body of desires and in terms of a more specific motivational structure goes deep. Plato himself abandoned the former for the latter: contrast the account in *Protagoras* with that of book 9 of *Republic*, where he describes universal tyrannical desires that for reasons of character most people do not act on. Thanks to Eric Brown for pointing this out to me.

The Nietzsche quotation is a composite of two passages from *Beyond Good and Evil*, on pages 473 and 299 of the Kaufmann translation. (Reprinted in *Basic Writings of Nietzsche*, New York, Modern Library, 1968.) In writing this book, I reread that work and also *The Genealogy of Morals*, which I had previously admired. I found both books repulsive. A lot of work has gone into rehabilitating Nietzsche from accusations of proto-fascism. The defenses are correct, intellectually. But try reading Nietzsche right after reading the witnesses to twentieth-century atrocity. The effect is chilling.

Images and emotions

A survey of recent work on emotional intelligence is Joseph Ciarrochi, Joseph P. Forgas, and John D. Mayer (eds), *Emotional Intelligence in Everyday Life*,

New York, Psychology Press, 2001. A classic on the rationality of the emotions is Ronald de Sousa, *The Rationality of Emotion*, Cambridge, MA, MIT Press, 1987. See also Ronald de Sousa and Adam Morton, "Emotional truth/emotional accuracy," *Proceedings of the Aristotelian Society*, supplementary volume 76, 2002, pp. 247–75.

TWO   THE BARRIER THEORY OF EVIL

Violence

For theories and data about how a person becomes violent see Lonnie Athens' *Violent Acts and Actors Revisited*, Chicago, University of Illinois Press, 1997; Richard Rhodes, *Why They Kill*, New York, Vintage, 2000; chapter 8 of Roy C. Baumeister, *Evil: inside human violence and cruelty*, New York, W. H. Freeman, 1997; and Jonathan Shay, *Achilles in Vietnam: combat trauma and the undoing of character*, New York, Maxwell Macmillan, 1994.

Transitions

Turiel's distinction is made in *The Development of Social Knowledge: morality and convention*, Cambridge, Cambridge University Press, 1983. See also Shaun Nichols, "Norms with feeling: towards a psychological account of moral judgment," *Cognition*, 84, 2002, pp. 221–36. Turiel and Nichols both refer to the distinction as that between the conventional and the moral, but this begs important questions, since some conventions have moral force. It is really between arbitrary conventions and moral principles with non-conventional roots. Blair's work is found in R. J. R. Blair, "A cognitive developmental approach to morality: investigating the psychopath," *Cognition*, 57, 1995, pp. 1–29.

My model of the approach to thresholds is suggested by a branch of non-linear mechanics called "catastrophe theory." For a non-technical exposition that highlights the aspect I am using, see Christopher Zeeman, "Catastrophe theory," *Scientific American*, 4, 1976, pp. 65–83. I am also influenced by the literature in evolutionary psychology. See Jerome H. Barkow, Leda Cosmida, and John Tooby, *The Adapted Mind: evolutionary psychology and the development of culture*, Oxford, Oxford University Press, 1992. There are game theoretical aspects to transitions to violence. If some individuals are capable of violence, then it becomes necessary for others to have that capacity, even if non-violent interaction is better for both parties. On the other hand, mutual knowledge that all parties have the capacity makes it less likely that the capacity will be actualized.

The quotation is from page 120 of Joe Simpson, *This Game of Ghosts*, New York, Vintage Books, 1994. Most of the book is relevant to the issues of this section: see also pages 87, 107, 150–1, 232, 321–3.

None of my discussion of processes of violentization should be taken to deny that some violent individuals are neurologically different from others. Rita Carter's *Mapping the Mind* (London, Weidenfeld & Nicolson, 1998) describes several pathologies, particularly frontal lobe damage, that are correlated with violence. A complicating factor is that traumatic experiences can inflict irreversible neurological damage.

Sociopaths

The quotes are from the *Diagnostic and Statistical Manual of Mental Disorders*, Washington, DC, American Psychiatric Association, 1980. Its "definition" of sociopathy is a bundle of characteristics which have some loose association with one another. I have emphasized the failures of empathy rather than tendencies to violence and impulsiveness. The terminology of "psychopath," "sociopathy," and "anti-social personality" is still very confused. Blair's work was based on a study of criminals classified as being violent psychopaths. Probably many of the subjects were both violent and sociopathic. No doubt they were also very varied in their individual psychologies.

I first met this quotation in Amélie Rorty's *The Many Faces of Evil*, New York, Routledge, 2001, which is a valuable source-book on many kinds of evil.

For recent moral philosophy that makes moral competence depend much less on knowledge of explicit rules see Stanley Clarke and Evan Simpson (eds), *Anti-theory in Ethics and Moral Conservatism*, Albany, SUNY Press, 1989, and Philippa Foot, *Virtues and Vices*, Oxford, Blackwell, 1978.

The barrier theory of evil

My account in this section is influenced by the work of Eve Garrard. See her "Evil as an explanatory concept," *The Monist*, 85, 2002, pp. 320–36. Garrard acknowledges the influence of John MacDowell. See his "Virtue and reason" in Roger Crisp and Michael Slote (eds), *Virtue Ethics*, Oxford, Oxford University Press, 1997, pp 142–62.

We apply "evil" to acts, their consequences, their motives, character, and whole people. I am focusing on acts, but acts taken as including their motives, so that, as an attribute of acts, "evil" is like "deliberate," "hurried," or "precise."

The filters that exclude evil options exclude many other options too. A central reason why we need to filter the options we think seriously about is simply that we are not intelligent or rational enough to consider all the things we could do.

David Brion Davis, *The Problem of Slavery in Western Culture* (Oxford, Oxford University Press, 1988) discusses how slave owners failed to see the nature of their actions. The quotation from Arendt is from *Eichmann in Jerusalem*, New York, Viking Press, 1963, p. 150.

In this chapter I use a variety of metaphors for the ways in which a barrier can cease to obstruct one: circumventing, overcoming, eroding. Each one seems apt for a different kind of evil so I have not stuck to any one consistently.

Small-scale evil

The law school injustice example comes from chapter 5 of Claudia Card, *The Atrocity Paradigm*, New York, Oxford University Press, 2002. I discuss Card's account of how to balance between evil and injustice in "Inequity/iniquity: Card on balancing justice and evil," *Hypatia* 19.4, 2004. I could cite Augustine, though controversially, in support of the evil-like quality of some lesser wrongs, in his deliberate use of a pointless petty theft rather than murder as his central example.

Real evil

On the explanatory force of moral attributions see Nicholas Sturgeon, "Moral explanations" in Geoffrey Sayre-McCord (ed.), *Essays on Moral Realism*, Ithaca, NY, Cornell University Press, 1988, pp. 229–55; Joshua Cohen, "The arc of the moral universe," *Philosophy and Public Affairs*, 26, 1997, pp. 91–134, which discusses the case of slavery; and chapter 4 of Adam Morton's *The Importance of Being Understood: folk psychology as ethics*, London, Routledge, 2002.

The reference to moral luck is to the discussion that began with Thomas Nagel and Bernard Williams' symposium "Moral luck," *Proceedings of the*

Aristotelian Society, supp. vol. 50, 1976, pp. 115–51. The upshot of the discussion is to undermine the idea that one's moral character cannot be a matter of the luck of when and where one lives.

Evil people, evil societies

The remark about Atta's character being noticed primarily by the women he encountered comes from a story in *The Guardian* newspaper, 5 September 2002.

THREE   NIGHTMARE PEOPLE

Serial killers

For the psychology of serial killers see Mark Seltzer, *Serial Killers*, London, Routledge, 1998; J. Norris, *Serial Killers: the growing menace*, New York, Doubleday, 1988.

Insanity?

The quotation is from page 372 of Gitta Sereny, *Cries Unheard: the story of Mary Bell*, London, Macmillan, 1998. For a sense of how complex issues of criminal responsibility are see R. A. Duff, *Intention, Agency and Criminal Liability*, Oxford, Blackwell, 1990.

My information about the conditions of child soldiers comes mainly from Human Rights Watch. See their web site at www.hrw.org.

For a sense of the bewildering mixture of lucidity and confusion, and of normal and bizarre emotions, that can be found in people who have committed atrocious crimes, see the transcript of the police interview with Andrea Yates, after she had drowned her five children, available at www.chron.com/cs/CDA/story.hts/special/drownings/1266294.

State atrocity

Essential reading here are Hanna Arendt's *The Origins of Totalitarianism*, New York, Harcourt Brace & World, 1951, and *Eichmann in Jerusalem: a report on the banality of evil*, revised and enlarged edition, London, Penguin Books, 1963. Arendt's "Thinking and moral considerations: a lecture," *Social Research*, 38, 1971, though harder to read than the two books, gives a more provocative diagnosis in terms of a specific failure of imagination. A readable discussion of Arendt's thought is Patricia Altenbernd Johnson, *On Arendt*, Belmont, CA, Wadsworth, 2001. See also Peg Birmingham, "Holes of oblivion: the banality of radical evil," *Hypatia*, 18, 2003, pp. 80–103. Gitta Sereny's *Albert Speer: his battle with truth*, New York, Knopf, 1995, and *The German Trauma*, London, Penguin, 2000, give a picture complementary to Arendt's, and are based on extensive interviews. Also useful is Ervin Staub, *The Roots of Evil*, New Haven, CT, Yale University Press, 1989. Though impressionistic and unscholarly, the "Afterword" to Primo Levi's *If This is a Man* (London, Orion Press, 1959) makes a lot of sense on the topic of what we do not and perhaps cannot know about the origins of the Holocaust and anti-semitism. The quotation from Levi comes from an interview with Giorgio Segrè, reprinted in *The Voice of Memory: interviews 1961–1987*, New York, New Press, 2001.

A greater occasion for state-sponsored mass violence in a democracy state is provided when there is an economically dominant ethnic minority. But that is not the situation of most first world democracies. For an assessment of the dangers here see Amy Chua, *World on Fire: how exporting free market democracy breeds ethnic hatred and global instability*, New York, Doubleday, 2002.

Terrorists

For Gandhi's philosophy of satyāagraha, non-violence, see M. Juergensmeyer, *Fighting with Gandhi*, San Francisco, Harper & Row, 1984. Gandhi was of course influenced by earlier thinkers, such as Tolstoy and Thoreau, as well as by Christianity. But Gandhi saw how to make it work.

The "God or Reason" point connects with the issues discussed in the "real evil" section of chapter two. The Cohen and Sturgeon papers referred to in the notes for that section are equally relevant here.

There is an extensive literature on moral dilemmas, situations in which there are moral objections to all one's options. See Walter Sinnot-Armstrong, *Moral Dilemmas*, Oxford, Blackwell, 1988. There is a general connection between moral dilemmas and evil in that moral dilemmas arise when the normal filters exclude all one's actions, so that to act at all one has to suspend the filters, thus opening the possibility of doing something evil.

Fiction versus reality

Ruth Rendell's *Master of the Moor* is a depiction of a serial killer from within the traditional detective fiction format. It pays very little attention to the motives of the killer, though.

I am simplifying a very subtle literature on the contrasts between explanations by simulation and explanations by theory. Good explanations of the issues are found in the introductions to Martin Davies and Tony Stone's two collections on the topic, *Folk Psychology: the theory of mind debate*, and *Mental Simulation: evaluations and applications*, both Oxford, Blackwell, 1995.

The Eliza program was the creation of the computer scientist Joseph Weizenbaum in 1966. It was meant to mimic the conversational patterns of a psychiatrist. There have been many imitations and variations since.

The possibility that the image of the serial killer influences the behavior of killers is discussed in chapter 8 of Roy Baumeister, *Evil: inside human violence and cruelty*, New York, Freeman, 1997. The mutual influence of real and depicted violence is explored in Alejandro Amenabar's 1996 film *Thesis*.

Matching images

The quotation is from page 112 of François Bizot, *The Gate*, translated by Euan Cameron, New York, Alfred A. Knopf, 2003.

FOUR   FACING EVIL: RECONCILIATION

Introduction

The relation between the moral powers of victims and the obligations of perpetrators is developed in chapters 8 and 9 of Claudia Card, *The Atrocity Paradigm*, New York, Oxford University Press, 2002.

The general line of this chapter contrasts with that of John Kekes, *Facing Evil*, Princeton, NJ, Princeton University Press, 1990. Kekes and I agree that the recognition that evil is different from other wrongdoing has a profound effect on one's moral attitudes. He argues for a generally retributive attitude, though. I think that he in a way underestimates how different some evil is from ordinary wrong: so different that the demand for retribution could never be satisfied.

Intuitive understanding

In my *The Importance of Being Understood: folk psychology as ethics* (London, Routledge, 2002), I try to link our capacity for intuitively understanding others to our capacity for shared practical activity. In my picture, the basic skill is that of imagining the actions, and the feelings that go with them, when several people do something together. But my argument in this chapter doesn't require you to buy that. Most of what I say could be expressed in terms of the extreme opposite theory, in which to understand an action is to deduce it from a general theory of rational action. See the works referred to in the notes to the "fiction versus reality" section of the previous chapter for the philosophical debate on intuitive understanding.

The example of the general came from a reflection on what it would be like *not* to act as General Colin Powell did at the end of the first Gulf War. Ronald Milo's *Immorality* was published by Princeton University Press in 1984.

Imagining evil

The Arendt quotation is from pp. 105–6 of *Eichmann in Jerusalem*.

The derivation of envy makes it a special case of what decision-theorists call "satisficing": using background knowledge to set a threshold and then being content to choose anything above that threshold. Satisficing, like filtering from all our options a few to ponder, is forced on us by our finiteness compared to the problems we face.

In exploration IV "Moral progress" of *The Importance of Being Understood*, I also described ways in which we could imagine evil actions. The aim there was to describe distinctly different ways in which we could think about our actions, while the aim here is to describe small useful tweakings of our imaginative capacities.

I have been slightly evasive here about what is explained or understood in the examples. The explanation is always partial, one understands why the person did some action rather than any of some range of alternatives. Typically, one has some understanding of the person's strategy for overcoming barriers to harm, but one does not understand where that strategy came from or why it persists.

Reconciliation: the South African case

Sources of information on the South African Truth and Reconciliation Commission are Desmond Mpilo Tutu, *No Future without Forgiveness*, New York, Doubleday, 1999; Kader Asmal, *Reconciliation through Truth*, New York, St Martin's Press, 1997; Deborah Posel and Graeme Simpson (eds), *Commissioning the Past: understanding South Africa's Truth and Reconciliation Commission*,

Johannesburg, Witwatersrand University Press, 2002. Essays in this last book are very helpful in addressing the question "what kind of truth was being aimed at?" Historical truths about the causes of complex social events are not likely to result from such commissions. The participation of Pik Botha is an exception to the absence of top government people. It is not at all clear what counted as showing contrition to the satisfaction of the Commission. I suspect a deep ambiguity here. The Commission's practical mandate was to achieve reconciliation, but as the title of Archbishop Tutu's book suggests, it was also driven by a possibly hopeless aim of achieving forgiveness. Information on other such commissions can be found at http://www.hrcr.org/

The Athenian precedent is discussed in John Atkinson, "Truth and reconciliation the Athenian way," *Acta Classica*, 42, 1995, pp. 5–13; and Nicole Loraux, *The Divided City*, New York, Zone Books, 2002.

Murder Victims' Families for Reconciliation maintains a website at www.mvfr.org.

Reconciliation versus forgiveness

In everyday life we speak of "moving on" from emotions of rage. I have been influenced by a draft paper of Robin May Schott making philosophical sense of this idea. It will appear with other papers on Claudia Card's work in *Hypatia* 19.4, 2004.

There is an extensive literature on the connections between emotions in the shame/remorse/guilt family. See Gabriele Taylor, *Pride, Shame, and Guilt: emotions of self-assessment*, Oxford, Oxford University Press, 1985; Patricia Greenspan, *Practical Guilt: moral dilemmas, emotions, and social norms*, New York, Oxford University Press, 1995. When words in these and other such families are used, they usually mark several contrasts simultaneously. The contrasts I am choosing to focus on are not the only ones. There is a lot more to say about the way everyday explanatory and moral discourse uses simultaneous contrasts between members of small families of words to make a large number of fine-grained distinctions between states of mind.

The Mandela quote is from his Preface to Deborah Posel and Graeme Simpson (eds), *Commissioning the Past: understanding South Africa's Truth and Reconciliation Commission*, Johannesburg, Witwatersrand University Press, 2002.

One-sided reconciliation

The quotation from Primo Levi is on p. 106 of *The Voice of Memory*. Levi is referring to a theme of *If This is a Man*.

Evil-resistant institutions?

The "courts" I am imagining would be closer to coroner's courts than criminal or civil courts. Perhaps they would be better organized around a continental-style presiding jurist than around an adversarial process. As I write, the UK home secretary is considering courts of "restorative justice" that would have some resemblance to my proposal.

Given the role high-flown rhetoric and obscure doctrine often play in large-scale evil (and in the self-justifications of smaller-scale perpetrators), I considered ending the book with an argument for the need for satire and irreverence. Pythons to the rescue. But I felt that many readers would not respond well to this. Irreverence is not given the respect it deserves.

Index

CPSIA information can be obtained at www.ICGtesting.com
Printed in the USA
LVOW072322270412

279325LV00005B/8/P